American *Conversations*

Edited by
Richard Maidment

Hodder & Stoughton

in association with

The Open University

Acknowledgements

The author and publishers would like to thank the following for permission to reproduce material in this volume:

David Brower photo courtesy of Range/Bettmann/UPI; Noam Chomsky photo © Donna Coveney; J K Galbraith photo © Jim Kallett; Henry Kissinger photo © Bachrach; Walter Mosley interview reprinted by permission of the author and the Watkins/Loomis Agency; Walter Mosley photo courtesy of Serpent's Tail; Arthur Schlesinger jr. photo © Dominique Nabokov; Hugh Sidey photo courtesy of *Time Magazine*. Many thanks to all the interviewees who supplied their own photographs.

Every effort has been made to trace and acknowledge ownership of copyright. The publishers will be glad to make suitable arrangements with any copyright holders whom it has not been possible to contact.

British Library Cataloguing in Publication Data

Maidment, R. A.
  American Conversations
  I. Title
  973.92
ISBN 0 340 63091 4

First published 1995
Impression number   10 9 8 7 6 5 4 3 2 1
Year   1999 1998 1997 1996 1995

Typeset by Wearset, Boldon, Tyne & Wear.
Printed in Great Britain for Hodder & Stoughton Educational, a division of Hodder Headline Plc, 338 Euston Road, London NW1 3BH by Bath Press Ltd, Bath, Avon.

Preface

This book started life as a radio series. The radio programmes were produced for the Open University course, *The United States in the Twentieth Century* and were broadcast on BBC Radio 4. The idea behind the series was to offer a distinguished and interesting array of individuals the opportunity to reflect both on their own lives and on the American experience during the latter part of this century. The programmes were designed to explore the developments in American society and culture that have occurred over these past several decades. They were also designed to interweave the public with the private and offer a very personal and distinctive view on the momentous public events that have taken place during the interviewees' lives.

The participants in this project are a diverse group although they share one characteristic; they all have a distinguished record of achievement in their chosen career. Some of them are still in the process of establishing and defining their reputations, while others have had an active professional life spanning several decades. Collectively, they provide a unique perspective on a society which has seen remarkable changes in the course of the last half of this century:

Tom Bradley (p. 1) was the first African-American mayor of Los Angeles, where he served for three consecutive terms. He was also the first Black man to be nominated by a major party as a candidate for Governor of California. Although Bradley lost to the Republican candidate, he had a profound impact on California politics and on race relations.

David Brower (p. 11) was the founder of Friends of the Earth and has been one of the leading environmentalists in the United States over the last three decades.

Noam Chomsky (p. 19) is a Professor at the Massachusetts Institute of Technology. He has been the leading radical critic of American foreign policy since the 1960s. He is also an established authority in the field of linguistics.

John Kenneth Galbraith (p. 34) is one of the most distinguished economists in the United States. His books have frequently set the agenda for debate on economic policy. He has also been active in public life and was the US ambassador to India.

Henry Kissinger (p. 45) is a former National Security Adviser and Secretary of State. He won the Nobel Peace Prize and is widely considered to be one of the architects of American foreign policy in the years after the Vietnam War.

John Lewis (p. 54) is a member of the US House of Representatives from Georgia. He was a student civil rights leader in the 1950s and 1960s and was closely involved with Martin Luther King. He is committed to the principles of non-violence and integration.

Walter Mosley (p. 66) is a novelist, who writes in that distinctively American genre of 'hard-boiled detective' fiction. Mosley gives every indication of being as successful as the two authors he most admires, Raymond Chandler and Ross MacDonald. Intriguingly Mosley is both Black and Jewish and the issue of identity often surfaces in his novels.

Arthur Schlesinger jr. (p. 81) is perhaps the most eminent American historian of his generation. He won the Pulitzer prize for the *Age of Jackson* and his three-volume history of the New Deal is considered definitive. In *The Disuniting of America*, he reflects on multiculturalism and the question of an American identity.

Hugh Sidey (p. 91) has had a long and distinguished career in journalism. He joined the Washington bureau *of Time Magazine* in the 1950s and has used this vantage point to write about American political life. Sidey's column in *Time* is noted for its reflective and thoughtful quality.

Gloria Steinem (p. 106) is frequently described as the leading feminist of her generation. She helped to found *Ms Magazine* and her writings over the past three decades have made her an influential voice in the United States on issues concerning women.

Henry Waxman (p. 117) is a member of the US Congress. He represents the 24th District in California, which includes Beverly Hills and Hollywood. It is one of the most liberal districts in the United States and Waxman is one of the most powerful Democrats in the House of Representatives.

The radio series was broadcast in 1994 and I was delighted by the response to the programmes. As a result I felt that these conversations should be published, especially as the original interviews were considerably longer than the versions transmitted. This book contains the original transcripts, lightly edited in the cause of readability.

This book is the product of a collective enterprise. I owe a considerable obligation to several people, but my greatest debt is to those who agreed to be interviewed. They all have exceptionally busy lives, yet they gave their time willingly and generously to this project. I am very grateful to all of them.

I wish to thank all of my colleagues on the course team which produced *The United States in the Twentieth Century*. They were consistently very supportive and helpful. I have a particular debt to Jeremy Cooper of the BBC who was the producer of the radio series. The success of the programmes are due in no small part to his abilities and skills. Grahame Thompson, my colleague in the Faculty of Social Sciences at the Open University, conducted the illuminating interviews with Noam Chomsky and John Kenneth Galbraith. The enthusiasm and energy of Val Price, of the BBC, kept the project going whenever it was in danger of flagging. Giles Clark of the Book Trade Department at the Open University, took care of all the details of turning the radio series into a book. Anne Hunt prepared the manuscript with her usual skill and her ability to detect and then rectify my mistakes. Finally I would like to thank Juliet Pope who gave me the idea of turning the radio series into a book and also for her help with the interviews with Gloria Steinem and Walter Mosley.

Richard Maidment

Milton Keynes, December 1994

Tom Bradley

Mayor Bradley, you've had a remarkable career. You've just left office, so how do you feel about it?

On July 1st 1993 I retired as mayor, after 20 years of service in that office. It was a culmination of a 52-year public service career. I started as a police officer in 1940 and then served 21 years in that capacity. Upon my retirement I began the practice of law; I had gone to night law school while I was in the department. I was approached by a group of business people who asked if I would run for city council, and I thought about it for three days and finally decided that public service had been my life and it was just natural to continue. So I ran for the city council, was elected, served there for 10 years prior to running for and being elected as mayor. It's been a wonderful 52-year career. All of the satisfaction, all of the challenges, all of the problems, all of the possibilities and joys that one gets from a very hectic life in public service. It has been a wonderful experience for me.

Where were you born and do you have any vivid memories of your childhood?

I was born in a little town called Calvert Texas, in the eastern part of Texas. It was a town of people, principally a cotton farming town. We left and came to California when I was seven and made one brief stop in Arizona on the way. I went back in 1976 when the town had a celebration for me when I had been elected mayor. I've been back twice since then. I have some relatives who still live in that community and I have some warm feelings. I've established a number of friendships in recent years with the mayor for example and some of the other people in town. The contrast between living in a small cotton town at Calvert Texas and where I am today is so different that you can't even appreciate it.

What are your first memories of Los Angeles?

I came to Los Angeles at the age of seven. It was looked upon by people who came from the rural sections of this country as the golden State, a land filled with opportunities, and a great life. Well, it

didn't exactly turn out that way in the beginning, but it was a
quantum leap from where I had been as a youngster growing up in
~~ated and very hostile territory of Calvert Texas. I think
nia as I did, had great visions for what life
most of us it didn't turn out that way in the
ook generations for some people to achieve
nich they had when they first came here.

:ult city for the African-American community?

a segregated city. There was a denial of rights
ases in most sections of the city. The
were limited. African Americans were
; to some of the most popular places at the
o to the swimming pools in town. Jobs were
and people just had to scratch their way out of
;, to build a better life for themselves and their
families. My ramily also arrived just before the Great Depression of
the thirties and if we thought times had been bad, we only had to wait
a few years until the Depression hit. I mean everybody was equal in
those days – equal in deprivation and denial, so we pretty much got
along well together. I went to integrated schools in the city, I was a
good scholar and athlete, and I did well in that regard. I was offered a
scholarship to the University of California at Los Angeles because of
my track and football prowess, and that opened a whole new world
for me. UCLA really is the dividing point in my life, because my
exposure to people and to opportunities at UCLA and thereafter
made the difference in my career and in my life.

Did you decide to join the police force after UCLA?

Yes, I decided that I wanted to begin making some money to help
take care of the financial obligations to my family. I also wanted to
get married and be able to take care of my wife and children. The
Police Department was the best paying civil service job in town, and I
actually went somewhat on a lark because some of my friends were
taking the examination one Saturday, and I said I'll go along with you.
I did, and I wound up top of that list and was appointed within a

3

matter of a couple of months. I had fully intended to serve two years and then go back into education and perhaps become a teacher. Well it didn't work out that way; I loved the job, I loved the experience and the opportunity which had been provided for me to work with juveniles – youngsters who needed some inspiration, some guidance, some direction in their lives. And I'm pleased to say that many of those young people see me on the street today and come up and thank me for what I did to help change their lives and to give them a new sense of direction.

When did you join the police force and what was it like for an African American in the LAPD?

I joined the Los Angeles Police Department in September 1940 and there were only about a hundred and three Blacks who were in the Department at that time. Segregation was awesome. You were not permitted to ride radio cars, nor permitted to work with White officers. Segregation was total. I stepped into that environment and the way I was able to relieve myself of the pressures and the concerns which I had about that system, was to throw myself into my work. I became a juvenile officer and served five years in that capacity. During that time I had a chance to get to know the Department, get to know many of the young people who I dealt with, and that gave me immense satisfaction. It helped overcome the problems that we were confronted with. There was an unwritten policy that no Black could rise above the rank of lieutenant, and having passed the promotional examination I became sergeant and then lieutenant, but it became clear to me that the unwritten policy was so firm, so severe, that there was no chance that I'd be able to advance in rank any further. I decided to go to law school and again that was a turning point in my career because the practice of law gave me access to many things I was denied.

How many years did you serve in the police force and when did you leave?

I served 21 years, and I retired in 1961.

Did the Police Department continue to be segregated and discriminatory?

Oh yes, I recall a number of conversations that I had with my superior officers and the captain of the division where I worked, when I tried to integrate the crews that worked for me. He was willing to try the experiment, but even before we could get it under way the one White officer who had agreed to become a member of this team, received such ugly pressure from his colleagues on the job that we had to abandon it for his own safety. I reminded the Captain and the Chief of Police that the system of segregation was not going to be broken until the Chief issued an order covering the entire department. I said if you issue that order, everyone on this Department will follow your lead. Chief Parker was a very strong administrator, he was feared by many, respected by most and if he said the word they would do it. Well, it was not until I was a member of the city council, which was several years later, in the mid–1960s that Chief Parker issued that order, which said there will be no discrimination with regard to assignments and places where people could work, or with whom the members of the Department could work. That was the breakthrough, it opened up opportunities for advancement. It permitted officers to work with each other and have respect for each other and thus translate that into having respect for the people they served. So it was a wonderful breakthrough and I've always been proud of that achievement ever since.

Tell me about your decisions to become a lawyer and enter public life.

I decided to run for the city council. I ran in a district which was very well integrated, about one third of the residents in that district were Black. This represented the breakthrough, because prior to that time hardly any city in this nation had been willing or able to elect a Black to such a position, except where the majority or a near majority of the constituency was Black. We had something to challenge us and something to prove. We showed that it could work, and that gave me the idea six years later in 1969 that I should try for mayor. LA was a city which at that time was only 17 per cent Black. It was almost unthinkable, at least that's what my friends told me when they tried to discourage me from running. But I have always been positive in my outlook and I thought it was possible. I'd made some friends. I'd been able to show my ability to serve all of the people, and I made a good run during the 1969 election. I came close but in the final days, the last two weeks of the campaign, the incumbent Mayor and his campaign became so ugly in their racist attacks and their approach, that people were simply frightened out of their wits. They became afraid that the Mayor's predictions would come true and that Black Panthers would take over City Hall and and that all of the policemen would quit and leave town. It was an unbelievable kind of campaign. I lost in the final days of that election. My lead of over 17 per cent over my opponent finally crumbled, and in the closing days of the election, people became so terrified that they backed off and voted for my opponent. I decided on election night that never again would I let an election turn on the basis of people listening to the accusations or the charges by my opponent, and fall victim to that kind of racist campaign, simply because they didn't know me well enough. So I began the next morning working in every section of the city, getting acquainted with people, helping them. And four years later in 1973, when I decided to run again, my opponent, the same incumbent Mayor, tried the same tactic and it simply didn't work.

You must have expected the racism and the hostility, so why did you put yourself through the ordeal?

It may have been naïve on my part to believe that it was possible to overcome that kind of system, that kind of pattern of prejudice and discrimination. I really believe it and that's the reason I ran for office in the first place, and that's the reason I ran for mayor the first and the second time. I guess it took two shots at it before my belief really came true. I believe that this country would be better if people chose their elected leadership on the basis of confidence of ideas and programmes and not on the basis of where they were born, the colour of their skin or their sex. I'm pleased to say that I have seen this theory proven true in city after city, at every level of government and across this nation, and I'm proud of that. I think we're a better country for it.

Did you have particular policy objectives?

We had many public policies that ranged all the way from improved education to developing a rapid transit system. They were all very important to my mind. The ability of the business sector to work with government was another major objective and I'm pleased to say that we have seen most of our goals come to fruition.

What were the principal problems in Los Angeles when you became mayor in 1973?

There were major difficulties at the heart of the city. The downtown area was deteriorating by virtue of age and neglect and businesses were leaving town. I decided that we had to have a revitalisation effort and if it was going to work it had to start at the heart, which was downtown Los Angeles. I took some criticism for it, but that was my strategy and I called upon the business community to join in a partnership with City Hall to tackle these problems. They enthusiastically joined, and I'm pleased to say that the skyline of this city changed dramatically in the 20 years that I served as mayor. We do have a working partnership between the private sector, the business leaders and the leaders in City Hall.

I suppose at this point Los Angeles is seen as a city with very substantial ethnic and racial difficulties. Were those evident in 1973?

Oh, I think that we had the most diverse city in the whole world. And that's been true for 20 years. We have been able to appeal to people to get them to work and live and play together in relative peace and harmony. Only on a couple of occasions have we seen a departure from that. The riots of 1992, April and May, were the most dramatic departure from that tradition. A part of the diversity has been caused by the rapid rise in immigration from all parts of the world, from Mexico, Central and South America, but also from the Far East. This remains one of the great challenges facing the leadership of both the political and the private sector in the city. If we don't learn to work together and to appreciate each other, we don't learn to have mutual respect for each other, this whole city could unravel, and could come apart. I still have confidence that we can do this, but it's going to take sensitivity on the part of the leadership to accomplish this goal. So I think that will remain the major challenge of the latter part of this century and into the year 2000 and beyond.

Is this a difficult city to govern?

I didn't complain about the nature of the political system. We have what we call a strong council, weak mayor form of government. There are very few powers given to the mayor, and in order to accomplish your programmes, you have to do so by powers of your persuasion and your ability to reach the people with your message. There are many who think it would be better if we had a stronger mayor system of government. I think it would work better and it would be a lot easier to get some of the things done which you'd like to. But the current system was not a block to our abilities to do the many things that were done in the past 20 years. So I am going to leave that task, changing the Charter, to my successors and the business community who also have said that we need to change it.

You're identified as a strong Democrat. Was that an asset or a potential weakness when you were mayor?

Ours has been a non-partisan system of government at city level for as long as I can remember. It is a tradition that goes back into the late twenties, and so in serving you would never know whether the mayor was Republican or Democrat. I didn't believe in using a divisive approach and since the law didn't permit us to run based upon our political affiliation, I didn't and I tried to serve all of the people fairly and well. I still think it's the best system of government for a local city. Partisan politics can enter at the other levels, state or national, but leave the cities to this non-partisan approach.

Was it of great symbolic importance that an African American became mayor of Los Angeles, a symbol to both the White and the non-White communities?

There's no question about it, it was a major breakthrough. The Superintendent of Public Construction in California – an African American – said to me that if I had not run for mayor it would have been impossible for him to run State wide as Superintendent of Public Construction. Mayors all over the country have said to me that my victory was the classic breakthrough of an old stereotype that Blacks or minorities could only be elected and only serve in an area where their constituency was either a majority or close to a majority of the population. I had never believed in that philosophy and set out to try to demonstrate that it was false. And it did have a monumental impact on this nation.

Do you think it had a particular impact on the Black community in Los Angeles by encouraging their aspirations and their belief that African Americans can succeed?

They appreciated the fact that doors which had been closed to them at City Hall finally had been opened. Jobs and contracts and other opportunities were now open to them when prior to my election they were closed. So it did represent a major source of increased power and opportunity for Blacks in this city. But it also was a matter of considerable pride, especially by young people, and this was true among all races and groups. Wherever I travel in the country, people, youngsters, 8, 10, 12, 14, 16 years old, would say 'I'm so glad you're our mayor'. And I'd ask them 'where are you from?' They'd tell me somewhere in Virginia, Ohio, or South Carolina. They identified with my victory because it gave them hope that it was possible for them to achieve their hopes and dreams, because Tom Bradley achieved them both for himself and for all of us in Los Angeles.

What was your greatest achievement as mayor?

I think the thing that stands out in my mind is the Olympic Games of 1984. It took enormous courage to try to do it in the face of the financial difficulties suffered in prior Olympics. It made a $3 billion economic impact on the Los Angeles community. We did not use a dime of public taxpayers' money, we did it with a privately promoted Olympic games, and we wound up not with a deficit as they had predicted, but with a surplus of $215 million. And that was divided between the International Olympic Committee (IOC), the city of Los Angeles and the US Olympic Committee. Youth and sports were the beneficiaries of those moneys.

Were you enormously saddened by the riots in 1992?

Yes I was, because I felt that there was always a possibility that there would be a negative reaction based on the shocking not-guilty verdict for the four officers who were charged with beating Rodney King. But it became apparent, shortly after the initial outrage, that it was an unthinking resort to violence, and the people that suffered most lived in the neighbourhoods where the worst rioting, burning and looting took place.

As you reflect on a distinguished career, do you feel there are some things that you did not accomplish or do you feel a real sense of satisfaction and achievement?

Well I ran for governor twice and in 1982 came within 52,000 votes, out of eight million cast, of being elected Governor of the State of California. That would have been another major achievement and another breakthrough that I thought was important. I fell short but I didn't waste any time grousing about, I went to work the next morning in what I said was the best job in this state and that was mayor of Los Angeles. So you might say that was a disappointment because I ran for the office, I was serious about it. I didn't make it the second time which was even more difficult but I tried it again, and didn't make it. So I might say that I'm sorry I didn't get elected, but when you look at the whole picture, when I woke up the next morning after that election night defeat, I couldn't have found a better job than mayor of Los Angeles.

Tom Bradley, thank you very much.

David Brower

Tell us a little about the environmental movement in the United States.

In the United States I keep being accused of having founded the environmental movement and of being the grandfather of it, and I say that at very best, I am the grandson. One of the people who contributed a great deal to it was John Muir, who was born in Scotland. He came to the United States when he was a young man, and then, of course, Henry David Thoreau had a great deal to say about it. One of the first people to get into the conservation movement as such was Henry Perkins Marsh. There is a book about him called *The Versatile Vermonter*, and he was one of the people who was concerned about what was happening to the Earth. We didn't get an environmental movement fully understood until the Theodore Roosevelt administration, where the conservation movement as such got its name and its beginnings. That was the early part of this century. The movement grew slowly. There had been some dedication of lands, setting aside lands that needed protecting, forests, National Parks. The first National Park was Yosemite in 1864, Yellowstone followed eight years later. The major forest reserves began in 1891. The Forest Service itself started in 1905, and National Park Service in 1916. The movement limped along without any great concern about pollution as such, until about 1970, except there were concerns about that, and I know I was a participant in some of the concerns during the mid-fifties.

In the thirties, in particular, you were involved in the Sierra Club.

Yes. I started getting involved with the Sierra Club in 1933, largely through mountaineering. I'd been doing some climbing when very young and late teens. I'd been leading people up easy peaks and one of the people I'd led up said I should get in touch with the Sierra Club. I did. I started reading their early bulletins. The Sierra Club started in 1892 and its *Bulletin* in 1893, and I bought the early issues and read those. There was a great deal about mountaineering but conservation was also featured. I got into the Club, primarily, to do my rock climbing in a more sensible way than I had been doing on my own. I learned a great deal about mountaineering during this period and entered a phase of mountaineering in my life that was important to whatever I was going to do. Mountaineers have to learn to accept a certain amount of risk and I think I learned the value of boldness that Geothe was alluding to in his quote, 'Whatever you can do or dream you can, begin it. Boldness has genius, power and magic in it' and that is, I guess, part of my religion. As to the rest of it, my religion, I am a drop-out Presbyterian. But I learned a great deal from William H. Murray, the Scottish mountaineer who wrote about commitment. He came up with the lines, 'Until one is committed, there is always hesitation, the chance to fall back always an effectiveness. But if one fully commits oneself', he said, 'providence moves too and all sorts of events and happenings happen that wouldn't otherwise come your way' and that's where he expressed his admiration for Geothe's couplet, and I found that to happen to me, is that providence, or whatever, once you commit yourself, things begin to fall in place. And I like that, and I guess I'll stick with that idea, that commitment is very helpful.

Tell me about some of the earliest commitments you made in the campaigning sense.

Well, the earliest major commitment I made was when I was in the Sierra Club and had been a member for, I guess, four or five years. The struggle started because the government intended to take part of the forest service lands and the Sierra Nevada and the King's River watershed and turn them into a National Park. Two of the major conservation organisations of the time, the Wilderness Society and the National Parks Association, were against the park. They were against it because it wasn't taking in all the land that they thought should be protected. Two of the most important canyons of the Kings River system were the South Fork Canyon and Tohippidy Canyon. These were destined for major dams, and we could not get support to include them in the park. However, we could include the rest of the High Sierra, which we loved in the Sierra Club. So without the help of the other organisations and the opposition of the Forest Service and the Chambers of Commerce, we nevertheless prevailed, and the Sierra Club was still a very small outfit. We only had about 3,000 members, but we stuck with it and we got a National Park, in 1940. We got those two canyons added about 15 years later, and had some more ideas about what still to add, so that if you can't get it all right away, at least get what you can and then go after the rest. My next big battle, when the Sierra Club began to get known in the nation as a whole, was over the supposed dams for a Dinosaur National Monument as part of the National Parks system. Two dams, Echo Park Dam, and Split Mountain Dam, were proposed, but the Park Service was not in a position to defend its own area. One of the Sierra Club advisers had said that this was just sagebrush country, but one of our members, who was then in his seventies, took his family down in riverboats through the Canyons and took a motion picture. The motion picture woke me up and we got into the battle, and I hadn't intended to be the leader of the battle, but that's the way it ended up, and there are no dams in Dinosaur.

What form did the battle take?

The battle took the form of bringing the public into the battle and letting people know what was there. We did a book, we published in magazines and we involved the public as a whole. But the Bureau of Reclamation, which was proposing the dam, said that the worst thing they had to contend with was a film we made called *Wilderness River Trail*. The film encouraged a good many people (200 people from the Sierra Club) in expeditions about 65 or so each, to take a one-week trip down through the canyons. We had 200 people of all ages, going down this river which had been said to be so dangerous that nobody could go down it. We took old people and young people down safely and made the film. We showed it all over the country, and that made quite a difference. In addition we were legislatively active, going to Congress, testifying at every opportunity, and pointing out what the alternatives were. The major dam at Echo Park, was supposed to save a lot of evaporation. The canyon would be deep and there would be little water surface to evaporate. I was able, by good luck, to go over their figures and find them wrong, and when the battle was over, the head of the Bureau of Reclamation for that region, was awarded a rubber sliderule for stretching the truth.

Tell me about the origins of Friends of the Earth.

Friends of the Earth happened because the Sierra Club got a little weary of David Brower as Executive Director. There were very many reasons why they should have got weary of me, because they had a good many places where I could excel in incompetence, but they went along with all that until I began to object to something that had been approved by the Board of Directors. It involved the development of nuclear power on the California coast. I was not yet against nuclear power, but I resented their trying to build reactors along one of the last undeveloped portions of the coast, and began to work against that as an employee of the Sierra Club. I was working against what the majority of the Board had voted for. I tried to change the attitude of the Board as well as I could. I myself ran for the Board of Directors. I'd been on it before I became Executive Director. So I thought I'd better run for the board in order that I could make motions and argue in the debates. I ran with a slate of four others. Our slate lost heavily in the election, and I had really no choice but to resign. As I did not want to get out of the environmental movement, I thought, I should start another outfit. So I thought of Friends of the Earth. My wife came up with the name, and then on July 11th 1969, it was incorporated in the State of New York, and we began our work. The things I wanted to do in Friends of the Earth were those that had bothered the Sierra Club. I wanted to have a good nuclear policy. I wanted us to be international, I wanted us to be public, and I wanted us to be legislatively active wherever we were. And that's what happened. So it started in the United States and then began to spread. France, England, Sweden, and then other countries came on, and at this point, Friends of the Earth International is in 51 countries, and in each of these countries, the organisation is independent. They each have their own Board of Directors but follow a general philosophical attitude that the Earth is to save and not to spend. We can get rid of wildness but, it is hard to reconstitute it, particularly if that wildness consists of a species. If you extinguish it, that is it. There is no rebuilding that species. A world is once in a planet's history and I've gone through various attempts to explain to the public how important

wildness is, and now I'd like to get it through the corporate mindset as well.

How are you setting about that?

Well, one of the things we are trying to do is to find some corporations that are getting the idea, and celebrating and rewarding them for what they've done. We point out that there will be no profit, no markets, no corporations, no factories, no anything on a dead planet. And we are killing the planet. We can list the things that we have done to the planet, particularly since the industrial revolution which started roughly 250 years ago. We were getting along reasonably well before that. We had a population of human beings that the Earth could probably sustain at the start of that industrial revolution. Certainly, we had one at the start of agriculture, which is only 10,000 years ago. Because we began to get so smart that we didn't value what the Earth had to offer and we still don't know how to put a value on the Earth itself. The economists haven't taught us that. My hope now is that if we build back what we've trashed, we'll learn how much value there was in it in the first place. I hope we do.

How easy is it to get your message across in the United States?

Well, one of the things that is supposed to help us in America is freedom of press, and more recently, freedom of information. In theory, we do not believe in government secrecy, but we practise it. Nevertheless, we have a Freedom of Information Act where we can ask the government, and the government is required to respond. The government is finding various ways to avoid it, if possible, or to put a price on it, something that you can't afford to pay, but in any event, we have access to information that I think is about as good as there is on the Earth, and we intend to get it. I would like to see freedom of information applied to the press, so that they felt free about repeating the information they know.

How well informed do you think the American population is now about the environment? Has there really been that big a shift in public opinion?

In America there has not been enough information on the environment to inform the public at present. And we had two administrations, 12 years under Presidents Reagan and Bush, where the environmental concern was not well publicised. It was different when the administration was fighting against us every foot of the way. We are *not* getting the information the public needs to be aware of what's happening. If indeed the GATT, the General Agreement on Tariff and Trade, is passed it will defeat the environmental gains of the last century. The press should be at least reporting that view. But the press doesn't do that either editorially, or in the news columns. The papers just go on selling the GATT. And it is a terribly important threat to the Earth. You know, we'll just keep hammering away and trying to get that story through.

To what extent do the American people think differently now? Has there been a real change in that sense?

In America, we've had some polls that are very encouraging. Something like 65 per cent of the people are willing to see economic growth slowed down, stopped if necessary, or jobs lost, in order to save the environment. So we see that in the polls. But we will get to other things that will just negate that view completely. Right now we are having a great struggle, because of unemployment, because of the recession, that I don't think is going to end until we have better understanding of what keeps an economy going. We are not getting the information we need to correct this. The public doesn't know as much as it needs. At this point I would say that if we tried to get a wilderness system set up, we would have a very difficult time. We had a freer flow of information in the 1960s than we have in the 1990s. It was fairly free in the 1970s, but then it just began to fade out. The bureaucratic and the corporate resistance have undone the opportunity to stop the rate at which the environment gets worse. We need to treat the Earth as a biosphere reserve in the universe and one of the things I think important that we realise, each of us, that we are brief tenants. We do not really own anything. We are just here for a short time, some of us shorter than others, and we need to have a new respect for the biological diversity of the Earth. Whoever owns

17

property, I think, should make sure that whatever he or she does on that property during the brief tenancy, does not diminish the biological diversity of that piece of land, and provide somehow for public access, not for everybody at once, but for some people, some time. I think you are doing some of that in England. That's important. I think that needs to happen, and if that were to happen, this would anticipate a point that a friend of mine made recently, where he was attending a conservation meeting, where they were trying to decide what else to save. He said, 'That's the wrong question. Don't ask what else do you want to save. What else do you want to trash?' And I think if the question is put that way, people will think twice and realise they don't really want to trash anything any more if they can help it. I think the list would be a very short list. And that's a new attitude and a new approach. What else do you really want to trash? Haven't we done enough of that already? Can't we spend the next century or two putting things back into the repair shop, trying our best to fix, to restore, to renew, to regenerate. To use a slogan – 'It's healing time on Earth'. Indeed it is.

David Brower, thank you very much.

Noam Chomsky

Professor Chomsky, you've been a persistent and powerful critic of the media and exposed its role and importance in shaping perceptions of American foreign policy. Could you just describe the ways in which language has been used by the media?

I don't think there is anything profound about the use of language. The media and the intellectual community generally shape terminology to the interests of power. Pick any word and you'll find that almost any word of political discourse has two meanings. One, its dictionary meaning and the other, the meaning that's used for ideological warfare.

Take democracy, it has a dictionary meaning which means society is democratic, insofar as the population can participate in some meaningful way in decisions that affect the general public, or something of that sort. It also has an ideological meaning which says that a society is democratic as it is completely dominated by the business class. The general public are what Walter Lippman called spectators not participants, who occasionally are permitted to push a lever and then are supposed to go back to their spectator role.

According to the Western elite, if the general public do begin to enter into the political system, that's what is called a 'crisis of democracy', a crisis that has to be overcome and we overcome that crisis by returning the population to their apathy and obedience. There is, in fact, a well-reasoned theory that lies behind this view which is articulated at great length in the academic literature, which argues that people are not the best judges of their own interest. We the elite are the best judges of the people's interest, and for their benefit we've got to keep what Lippman called the ignorant and meddlesome outsiders in their proper place or else they'll be in trouble. Well, that's democracy.

We're supposed to be interested in market democracy, so let's take markets. According to the theory, which you teach your students in an economics class, free trade maximises the efficient use of resources and everybody is in favour of that, so naturally, we like markets. In the real world however, it bifurcates. No wealthy society, or successful developing society ever subjects itself to market discipline unless there happens to be some accidental and contingent advantage in it. You look at the history of England or the United States, or any other developed society, you find, without exception, that they developed by violating radically the principles of the market. If the United States in the 1820s had followed the principle about efficient use of resources, it would now be exporting fur. Instead, they set up high tariff areas to keep out cheap British exports and built the textile industry. The steel industry was treated the same way. Right up to the present day the policy continues with computers and semi-conductors. Britain has done exactly the same thing. Britain was in favour of free markets, until it started losing in the competition and then it closed off the Empire.

So markets are not for us. They're for other people. But we do impose market conditions on the poor. The Third World is forced, compelled to meet extreme market conditions. Right now, for example the IMF has delivered a report on Nicaragua imposing strict market conditions; conditions which, if imposed on the United States, would destroy the society, but Nicaragua has got to follow it because they've got to follow orders.

What do you think will be the impact of the emerging global media corporations?

The big media corporations work within the corporate world. Like any other corporations they sell a product to a market. The market is other businesses, namely advertisers and the product is the ignorant and meddlesome outsiders, the people. They work within the whole corporate system, but as they become more transnational, they pick up other interests. The same is true of General Motors or Daimler-Benz as there has been a radical acceleration of a long-term process of internationalisation of the economy and by now it's a huge phenomenon. Unregulated financial capital now is so enormous that it overwhelms even powerful states. In fact, the European Union couldn't defend its potential currency against it.

The foreign sales of transnational corporations are now greater than all of world trade, and what's called world trade is sort of a joke. I mean, what's called trade is, in part, transfers internal to a particular firm. In other words, centrally managed interchanges with a very visible hand. These institutions do develop their own interest and as the media conglomerates make this same move towards internationalisation, they will develop some of their same interests. So, if you take, say, the World Bank and the IMF, and GATT, and the G7 Executive, and so on, they're kind of a *de facto* world government that reflects, to a large extent, the interests of international corporations and finance, and the media will be part of that.

But what effect is this going to have, do you think, on American foreign policy?

Well, first of all, let's remember that it's not really new. The energy companies, for instance, have always been transnational and they have always been instruments of American foreign policy.

However, the scale is quite different now. Governments, even powerful governments, now have to ask rather serious questions about what the 14 trillion dollars in capital is going to do.

So, if Bill Clinton decides on a mild stimulus for the economy, he's got to count on the fact that there will be a slight reduction in sales of treasury securities and bonds, which will mean that interest rates go up, which in turn will have such an impact on the economy. In fact, this huge sum of capital floating around the world has certainly had an anti-growth effect. It's driven countries to special kinds of policies – deflationary, low growth, low wage economies. And that has an impact on foreign policy. So there are serious constraints. If the international investing community or big corporations don't like a foreign policy initiative they can act in various subtle ways to undermine it.

Now, that's not really something totally new, so in 1968, for example, and after the Tet Offensive in Vietnam, some American corporations decided that the Vietnam War was getting too costly and therefore needed to be liquidated. They essentially gave the orders for the government to terminate. They told Lyndon Johnson to step down and begin negotiations, and so on. That's more or less what happened.

The phenomenon now is considerably greater because the most significant change in the world order has been the breakdown of the international postwar economic system. And that set in motion all sorts of things like this transnationalisation of the economy and that's going to affect everything that governments do.

Something that is new is the end of the Cold War. What is going to be the effect of the end of US/Soviet rivalry?

Well, in fact, the effect is entirely predictable and was predicted. The Soviet Union was a deterrent to US actions, and the converse was true as well. Now that was not a symmetrical relation. The Soviet Union internally was much more brutal but externally was much more conservative.

The US is a global power, so Soviet intervention was around at the borders, but US intervention is and was everywhere. The decline of the Soviet Union was quickly recognised by US planners and commentators and now we're going to be more free to intervene anywhere we want. Furthermore, intervention will have to have new pretexts. From about 1917 to 1989 there was a reflex – you want to attack some country, OK, the Russians are coming. Before 1917, it was the British are coming or the Huns are coming or, you know, something like that. After 1989 you needed a new pretext and, in fact, both of these phenomena were visible instantly as George Bush celebrated the fall of the Berlin Wall, which ended the Cold War, by invading Panama. It was the first time in about 70 years that we invaded a country for some purpose other than to stop the Russians. I mean, a month after the Berlin Wall fell you couldn't get away with that. So we were defending ourselves from words of Hispanic narcotic traffickers led by the arch demon Manuel Noreiga, who had been our friend until a couple of years before. Reagan's Latin American specialist pointed out that this was the first time the US had been able to intervene without any concern over Soviet counteraction anywhere. So we were much freer to intervene.

The next big intervention was the Gulf War and as many commentators pointed out, the United States and Britain, the enforcers, wouldn't have dared to put half a million men in the desert,

10 years previously. This time they could do anything they wanted. They could use arbitrary force against a completely defenceless Third World power and they did it. That is a change and that will continue.

So you think these interventions will increase?

I don't know, but the United States think they're much freer and that is interesting. The Clinton administration in early October 1993 came out with a new policy on intervention. They said it's now a matter of choice. We do whatever we feel like and we're no longer constrained. Of course it's for good purposes but you know, that is standard rhetoric. On the other hand, there are other things which make it much less likely that they'll intervene. One is the transnationalisation of the economy means that the United States no longer has the economic base for intervention that it once had. Another is that the American population is extremely hostile to foreign military adventures. There's even a name for that. It's called the Vietnam Syndrome. It means people don't like torture and murder and so on. These acts are considered a disease, a sort of pathology.

Another factor, perhaps even more important; there are lots of other ways to strangle and destroy people. Economic measures of control are much more cost effective and much easier to use. Intervention is typically deployed in the Third World. We intervene against the weak. The poor countries are much poorer relative to the rich countries than they were 30 years ago and they are compelled to follow orders. The orders are to adopt structural adjustment policies which are guaranteed to turn you into a two-tiered society with a small sector of wealthy people and a huge mass of suffering people and there's nothing you can do about it. Under those conditions, it's very unlikely that the conditions for intervention will arise.

I wonder if you could say a little bit about the importance of the Vietnam War and its impact on the conduct of American foreign policy since the 1960s.

Well, it's complicated. First on the personal side, it didn't change my attitudes towards anything, but it did get me more involved in things and I felt that I couldn't sit on the side and just do other things any more at that point. But my attitudes were the same and my understanding has been the same back since childhood.

The Vietnam War had a complicated set of effects. For one thing I would not call it an American defeat, in fact it was a big American victory and to see why you have to look back at the planning record. The United States basically didn't care about Vietnam. It could have been on Mars for all the government cared. I mean, there was a lot of talk by Eisenhower and others about the rice and the tin, and so on, but that's just hot air. What they cared about was – what they always care about in the Third World – the threat of successful independent development. This was a potential virus that could infect others. There was great concern back in the 1950s and the early 1960s that there would be successful economic development in the Chinese region – China itself, North Vietnam, and so on, which would simply be picked up as a model elsewhere.

Well, when you have a virus, there's two things you do. First, you destroy the virus and secondly, you inoculate the potential people that might be infected and that's just what the US did, under Kennedy mainly. Kennedy escalated the war against the international terrorist regime in Vietnam. He escalated its direct aggression against South Vietnam and then it picked up and became a major war and it destroyed, by the time it was over, three countries. So the virus was destroyed. The chance of successful development coming from Vietnam is essentially zero for a long time to come.

Furthermore, they inoculated the region. In every country around, the United States enthusiastically backed brutal murderous terrorist regimes, the main one was Indonesia where the government killed maybe half a million or a million people and that led to complete euphoria in the West. I've viewed the coverage. It's mind boggling. You couldn't duplicate it in Nazi Germany. Well, maybe you could. But there was complete euphoria about the slaughter of 700,000 or so peasants – 'a boiling bloodbath' as *Time Magazine* called it – and the reason was it inoculated that country. They were not going to get in trouble. In fact, that was regarded at the time, by American liberals, as justification for the American war in Vietnam because the generals wouldn't have had the courage to cleanse their own society if we hadn't provided the shield.

The same thing happened in Thailand. The same thing happened in The Philippines and the same thing happened in South Korea. So you had tough, brutal regimes with varying degrees of brutality, which prevented the virus from spreading. Well, that's a victory. Now the US didn't win a total victory so it didn't reincorporate Vietnam back into its own. If you're a real totalitarian, unless you win a total victory, you consider it a defeat. But if you look at the major interests, the US won. It is now 18 years since the end of the war, and we are still punishing Vietnam for the crime of having stood up to us. In fact the US ideological system is so fantastic that it has succeeded in turning us into the victims of the Vietnamese.

You have suggested that the impact of the Vietnam War has led the American people to be very wary of involvement overseas.

The Vietnam War came at a time of considerable ferment, when the civil rights movement was already going on and there was community organising going on. The feminist movement was just about beginning, and the Vietnam War had a great impact on these events. It awakened lots of people to the realities of the world and it led to a crisis of democracy. The Vietnam War, among these other things, had created a much more active, aware and politicised public. And that has had a permanent effect. That hasn't changed. In fact you see it even in public opinion polls. So, for example, if you look at public opinion there is a sharp divide between the educated sector and the general public. Among the educated sector, almost universally the Vietnam War is seen as a noble crusade that failed. We entered with blundering efforts to do good and became a disaster.

Amongst the general public – it is astonishing to me – about 70 per cent of the public says the war was fundamentally and morally wrong. It was not a mistake. Now that separates 70 per cent of the public from virtually all of articulate opinion who say it was a mistake but not fundamentally and morally wrong. And that is what's called the Vietnam Syndrome. The general public is just out of control on this issue. A change took place and they will not accept random massacre and terror any longer, and that's had effects all over the place. In the 1960s, for the first time in American history after hundreds of years, it became possible to at least face the original sin. When I was a kid we played cowboys and Indians you know, we were the cowboys and we killed the Indians. The academic profession was lying through its teeth about what was going on. They denied the presence of an Indian civilisation. They had all the evidence for it. In the 1960s, for the first time, the general population began to recognise that there was some problem here and by now the academic profession has been forced to change it interpretations, the general public is concerned. These are big changes, psychic changes, cultural changes and they took hundreds of years, and they came after the Vietnam War.

Do you think there is something distinctive about American foreign policy and the way in which it is conducted?

Well, you know, any society has got its particularities, but I think the general themes are almost universal. Every society has some sort of structure of internal power. You know, there's no society that is democratic in terms of actual power. If you look at the structure of internal power and the institutions in which it is reflected, you will expect to find, and you do find, that State power is heavily influenced by the structure of domestic power. Foreign policy will, therefore, by and large, be in the interests of those with domestic power. I mean, that is an insight that Adam Smith made.

In the United States the structure of domestic power is, of course, different from other societies. It has always been different from the Soviet Union. The Soviet Union was dominated by a military and bureaucratic elite. It was a tyranny and a totalitarian state. In the United States domestic power is overwhelmingly held by the business community. Here, the United States is somewhat different from Europe. It has a much more class-conscious business community and a much more effective one. There are numerous historical reasons for that. Europe had a society and a culture that modern state capitalism had to grow out of. The United States didn't. The colonists exterminated the native population or drove them away. There was not much of an aristocracy and not much of a feudal system and so the society just developed quite differently in several ways. For instance, one thing the United States has is a very violent labour history compared with Europe and labour has not won rights in the United States that it has won in Europe.

The United States, as everybody knows, is the only industrial country without any healthcare system. There are several other differences. The public relations industry, which is a huge propaganda industry devoted to controlling the public mind, is an American invention. Other countries have since picked it up. The United States has operated in a different set of international circumstances. Over the last 50 years, the United States has been in a position that is unique in history. Never in history has there been a country with the global power of the United States in 1945. I mean, it owned half the world's wealth and it was militarily overwhelmingly superior. Under those conditions they were able to try to run and organise the world. That's something that no power previously had tried to do and that does give very definite particularities to American foreign policy.

Do you think there is any relationship between the spread of English and the spread of exploitative relationships and power?

Let me give you a trivial example which illustrates a wider point. I was recently reading an economic weekly in India which was describing the national plans of the Indian government. India is not a small country; it is not Nicaragua. The writer pointed out it is pointless to look at Indian government plans because they are just coming straight from the World Bank and the IMF in Washington and furthermore, the article pointed out that the wording and even the spelling of the Indian national plan is now American rather than in the British style which is the style that would be natural to an Indian bureaucrat. Well, why is that? Because it is coming out of Washington. US power is so enormous and, in fact, exercised through what are, in part, its agencies like the IMF and the World Bank, that even a big country like India is basically not only taking its orders but even giving them in the words and the spelling that come out of Washington. That is an indication of something much broader. Science is done in English. It's the international language, but it is nothing to do with English. It has to do with American power.

Do you think that the influence of an English speaking culture – Anglo-American culture – has peaked?

First of all I think the term Anglo-American is extremely misleading. It is an elephant and a fly, you know. I mean England has lived with the illusion of having a special relationship with the United States, but if you look at what American leaders say privately, it is quite different. So, if you look at the declassified internal record you find that advisers to President Kennedy were privately describing England as 'our lieutenant'; the fashionable word is 'partner' you know. The British are supposed to hear the fashionable word but from the US point of view it is lieutenant. And culturally that's increasingly the case. These are hard things to measure but my sense about Europe in general, not just England, is that it is much more under American cultural domination now than it has been in the past. So when you read the European press, increasingly, it is like reading yesterday's *New York Times* and *Washington Post*. In fact, in England in particular, you get a kind of subordination to American power that is sometimes just mind boggling.

I agree with that, but I am curious whether the power of English may have peaked. The fastest growing language is Spanish. There are strong, economic and social developments coming from the Far East. I just wonder whether these may upset a pattern of the domination of English speakers.

Spanish is growing, but that's the poor and they are not going to have a lot of influence. The Far East is a different story. It is Japan based, but insofar as there is an international language, it is probably English to a large extent. Japan and its periphery, its former colonies, are, culturally speaking, to a large extent under US influence. I have just come from teaching a class, in MIT Graduate School, and I would say half the students were Asian. They are coming here to study and that is standard. In the long term, they may become an independent force. Nothing is fixed in stone, you know, but I don't see any decline in US influence. In fact, in my opinion, the United States is probably more influential now than it was 10 or 15 years ago.

You have been a great champion of the underdog throughout your intellectual career but to some extent don't the powerful determine what can be said by the exploited? Isn't there a sort of paradox here?

There is. I mean, free speech. The people who founded the Chicago School, who pointed out that freedom without power, just like power without freedom is intolerable. And that is correct. I think it is important, crucially important, to defend freedom of speech and one of the best things about this country, in my opinion, is that it defends freedom of speech, I think uniquely in the world, much better than England and Canada, or any European country that I know of. And that's great. On the other hand, we should not overlook the fact that this is a capitalist country and in a semi-capitalist country everything is a commodity. Freedom is also a commodity. You get about as much as you can buy. So I have a lot of freedom of speech. A Black kid in Dorchester, downtown Boston, theoretically has freedom of speech, but in fact he doesn't. That is a reality which should be overcome.

I suffer from it too. One of the first books I wrote on the media, in fact, was published by a flourishing publisher which happened to be owned by a huge corporation, Warner Communications. They didn't like the book so they put the publisher out of business. They closed down the whole publisher and destroyed every book that it had. Well, you know, I had freedom of speech, of course, and since I'm privileged it didn't really bother me very much. I sent the book somewhere else but that power, that latent power, has an enormous effect on what actually happens. In the media it is just overwhelming.

Are you still banned from the Public Broadcasting System?

Well, there is no official ban. It's just that we have a deeply totalitarian strain in the culture, and critical and dissident voices are excluded but not by a ban. It operates through various informal devices. One thing that has been recognised, even in the academic profession, in the discussion of these issues is that the more free a society, the more you must control opinion for perfectly obvious reasons. If you can control people with a bludgeon you don't care much what they think. But if you can't control people with a bludgeon you'd better control what they think because they might cause you trouble. So in the Soviet Union probably three-quarters of the population listen to foreign broadcasts and maybe half the educated people read underground publications. In the United States nobody listens to foreign broadcasts and the dissident press reaches an insignificant percentage of the population. It is like noise on the periphery. I think that the media, and the intellectual community as well, are very careful to keep the gates tightly closed because of the dangers, in a free society, of letting people think.

Can I ask you about linguistics and your relationship to other sorts of schools of linguistics?

More generally, I would like to find out the truth about the world. There are different aspects of the world where we find out about the truth quite differently. I mean, certainly language is used in a social context. Everything we've been talking about is an example of that, but I believe, in my opinion there is nothing known about this topic that would stress the intelligence of a 10 year-old. It is all right on the surface. So it happens that they call me a linguist, but as far as the work I do on, say, international affairs and the media, I might as well be an algebraic topologist. There is no carry over.

My interest in linguistics comes from a totally different source. I'm interested in what human beings are, you know, what kind of creatures they are. And it turns out we can find out a lot about what kind of creatures they are by studying certain properties of the brain and we can learn about those properties of the brain by filtering out what are, in fact, irrelevancies from the point of view of those properties, namely the social context. There is no conflict between this and sociolinguistics.

It has been remarkable that you have been able to maintain such a breadth of interests. Do you think that is going to be possible in the future? Are we coming to an end of a period where people perhaps dabble in a whole range of areas? Is the specialist intellectual going to be the intellectual of the future?

I think in areas where there is real intellectual progress that's undoubtedly the case. I mean, let's take the wing of this building where we're now sitting, which happens to be the Linguistics Department. Say 15 years ago every Faculty member in the Department could play a constructive role in the dissertation work of every student. Now that's very far from true and it is not that we have got more stupid, it's just that the field has advanced so far that to really know the work that is going on in some particular area, you have to put an enormous amount of effort and attention to it. And what is happening in linguistics is also happening, to an even greater extent, in mathematics where a good mathematician may talk to only five people in the world. On the other hand, let's bear in mind that the number of areas where there is any deep understanding is extremely small. The understanding of most topics, including virtually all topics of direct human concern, is pretty much on the surface. I don't see the slightest indication that it is changing.

Finally can I ask you about American intellectuals? You are a critic of American intellectuals. Is there something particular and specific about being an intellectual in America?

Yes, there is something particular. They live in the most powerful country in the world, therefore what they do is more important. They happen to be in a very free society so, therefore, their civility and power, which is common to the intellectual classes, is much more dramatic. George Orwell wrote most interestingly, in my opinion, about England. If you look at the unpublished preface to *Animal Farm* it was a critique of a free society, British society, and that is far more interesting than *Animal Farm* itself which is a critique of the totalitarian state. The United States is a very free society, as well as a very powerful one and therefore the behaviour of the educated classes is of great significance, plus the fact that I happen to be here so it's what concerns me.

Noam Chomsky, thank you very much.

John Kenneth Galbraith

Professor Galbraith, you have had a long and distinguished career. The Great Depression of the late twenties and early thirties was a seminal moment in both American history and in your own intellectual and personal development. Can you describe what the American economy was like during that period and how you reacted to those events?

Well, I like that reference to 'the long and the seminal' and my economic career did, believe it or not, begin in the years of the Great Depression. And this was from a certain point of view, an economist's point of view which is rather significant because economists . . . were at the centre of things.

For the world at large, this was a period of dismal, continuing unemployment. Here in the United States the only safety net was the soup kitchen, the soup line, and I remember once I was doing a research project. I did my graduate work in California and I stayed at a hotel in the centre of Los Angeles, in a not particularly run-down part of the city and coming out in the morning, the impoverished people that had been sleeping in a nearby park would come hoping for some money.

I didn't have very much money but the notion that there were all these people dependent on charity, the most vulnerable kind of charity, for their next meal was one of the saddest recollections I have of that time. And this lasted for 10 full years. Yes, there were daily predictions that it would be over, certainly weekly predictions. As a matter of fact, it was so bad that when the Hoover administration predicted recovery, the stock market would turn down on the very logical theory that if things were getting better they wouldn't be making those predictions.

So, did this affect your own intellectual development?

Oh, quite clearly, first with a sense that the norm in economics, in economic behaviour, was not good times and full employment and that made me extremely susceptible to John Maynard Keynes and the notion of an underemployment equilibrium. It attracted me and all my generation. It provided an association between economic behaviour and human well-being, human happiness that I have ever since considered to be very close. And I think, and I don't want to praise myself unduly, I would hope that during those years I developed a certain sense of the problems of impoverishment, the problems of unemployment, the problems of the people, that are evident in our central cities. There was a sense of human despair that has been with me ever since.

Were you involved in any of the policy formulation of the New Deal?

I was deeply concerned in those days with agricultural matters and I was involved in various policy discussions, but until World War II at a very low level. I was in Washington a great deal but I don't wish to exaggerate. I was there in a far from pivotal position. I knew the people who were in pivotal roles, but I was not one of them.

Do you draw any parallels between the 1930s and the period of the mid-1970s, early 1980s? Are there any similarities between them?

Oh, sure. The great light at that time was Keynes who came with the notion that the modern economy could settle in, into an underemployment equilibrium – that was his phrase. This occured by the balancing of savings and investment which came about, not by the reduction of interest rates and capital becoming more available, but by the economy settling down to the point it forced an equilibrium. This was the heart of the Keynesian idea; it is still under some dispute.

And from that came continuing unemployment and continuing stagnation in the economy. The very important notion was that the modern economy doesn't find its norm at full employment. It's perfectly possible that it finds its norm at a high level of employment. We can see in the autumn of 1993 that there has been years of relative stagnation in the United States which is spreading out to other countries, including Britain, notably Britain, and one has to ask oneself whether this idea of an underemployment equilibrium isn't part of the system.

Presumably one would want to draw a distinction between a depression of, say, the thirties which was extremely deep and lengthy, with the shallow recession of the early 1990s. Would you say that the distinction between 'depression' and 'recession' is significant?

Oh, I would say this is something worth remembering. In the last century, the nineteenth century, when times were bad there was a reference to a panic and the word panic is rather frightening, so people came to say well it's not a panic, it's only a crisis. Marx then made the idea of a crisis very palatable, so after World War I in the United States, when things turned rather bad, people said well, this is not a crisis it's just a depression. The mildest possible term.

The word depression took on the connotation, of the Great Depression and people came to say well, economists came to say, well, not a depression, only a recession. And then, of course, a certain number who were committed to optimism have now said 'not a recession, it's just a growth adjustment'. This is purely verbal.

What we had in the 1930s was a long period of unemployment, a long period of underperformance in the economy and that is what we have now, although it isn't nearly as bad.

Looking back at the period after the New Deal, what role did you play during the war?

There's always a danger of exaggerating one's role but I think it's fair to say that I was one of the more important administrative figures in World War II economic policy. I was the Deputy Administrator of the Office of Price Administration in charge of prices. And you could lower a price without my permission in the republic but you couldn't raise a price. And that gave me a sense of power but unfortunately that gave me the feeling that my life has been in decline ever since.

When you were effectively the regulator of prices for such a vast economy, did this have any effect on your attitudes and opinions about economics?

Oh, that was a highly educative experience, no question about it, on a whole variety of matters. First, the power of special interests in the Congress. Anybody wanting a better price came to the Congress and the Congress came to me. I've often told the story, if it was cotton, they came to a southern legislator whose name was Cotton Ed Smith, and appealed for a high price for cotton. Cotton Ed then got in touch with his son, who happened to be clerk to the committee and who was called Boll Weevil Smith, and Boll Weevil then called me and I spent the next morning before the Senate Committee on Agriculture and Forestry.

And I had a continuing lesson, which has served me very well, on the intelligence quotient of the great industrial bureaucrat. If you had, in those days, spent a whole morning with the heads of the steel industry in the United States, you came away with a certain doubt as to whether we should be making steel or not. They were masters of the uninformed cliché, cited with enormous self-confidence. You asked them for something and you always got the same answer. Well, you can trust the patriotism of the American businessman. That patriotism usually involved a feeling that prices should be a little higher than they were.

Was the scepticism that you felt during this period the reason why you wrote subsequently about the importance and significance of big business?

The notion of the great corporation, the notion of the bureaucratic attitude, the notion of the power of, what I later came to call the techno-structure, goes back partly to that time, no question, although it also goes to scholars who wrote about that, Adolph Berle and Gardner Means, who possibly affected my thinking most over John Maynard Keynes, left the indelible imprint of the role of the 500 largest corporations on the American economy.

If we move on to the postwar period now. You mentioned the importance of Keynes in your own thinking, presumably this was a period of great optimism for you. This was also the period when you developed your work around the private affluence, public squalor

thesis. This is a rather pessimistic thesis about the consequences of the long boom. How did you handle this paradox?

There was no problem there. I have to step back a little bit. Like others, I shared, during the war years, a sense of pessimism as to what would happen after the war. Now, as the result of the long period of the depression in the 1930s, I came to believe from Keynes, that maybe the underemployment equilibrium was normal and I engaged in a lot of discussions during the war years about how we might correct that in the postwar period.

What happened was, of course, that we came out of the war with an enormous reservoir of spendable savings, a very strong supportive aspect to the economy, as compared with 1930s. The Korean War was also a stimulative influence as was the Marshall Plan. All of these factors brought us to relatively full employment and carried us along through the rest of the 1940s and the 1950s. I didn't foresee that but I welcomed it and that was part of the basis of my comment on the affluent society where I focused on the two things. One was the continuing islands of poverty in our mountain areas in the south and in the central cities and, additionally, the very great difference between our private well-being, as it was developing, and our public services. We were getting to the point where we had good radio and television but lousy schools. We had clean houses and filthy streets; we were losing control of the visual aspects of our environment – highways loaded with billboards concealing the landscape. A beautiful verse from that time went, 'I think that I shall never see a billboard lovely as a tree. I think unless the billboards fall I'll never see a tree at all.' It was just an incredible disproportion in our well-being that I dealt with in those years.

You have refined the thesis slightly differently around this idea of the culture of contentment. Could you just explain what the culture of contentment is and how it's linked to this public squalor/private affluence thesis?

Well, I suppose that one gets into a line of thought that is rescued only with difficulty and this was certainly part of the continuing concern of mine. The culture of contentment which I've dealt with more recently is the consolidation of political power both in Britain and the United States, in the hands of the most comfortable and contented of the people. It isn't the old-fashioned capitalist; the old dialectic of capital versus labour we can put aside. It is no longer central.

The modern dialectic is between a large community of businessmen, business bureaucrats, business managers, professional people, academic people, lawyers, physicians, all of whom have a relatively comfortable existence, who have no great complaint about the nature of the modern society, and the people who are outside – the underclass – the people who live south of the Thames in London. The people that live in Harlem, South Bronx in New York, and in South Central Los Angeles. The people who are voiceless in the system but do a great deal of the work that makes life for the rest of us possible. And it was that dialectic, that conflict that I sought to deal with, which was emerging in my mind at the time of the affluent society, which I have sought to do some work on since.

How do you react to the argument that this so called contented minority are not that content and that they are forced to suffer higher taxes etc? They're not content at all. They seem to be very discontented.

Oh no. I don't think that's true for a moment. I think on the whole they find their life very good. They express their discontent vigorously, vividly, sometimes profanely, when they see the threat of taxation coming, which might be necessary for help to the underprivileged, to those outside. That is when they do express their discontent. That is when they get angry. And I find that true even of some of my friends.

Could I make a rather general point about the importance you attribute to money and the financial system. Why is money in the financial system so important?

There are several answers to that. First, that we have an exaggerated view of the financial world and the people in it. There's a deep instinct that there is some association between intelligence and money. There's a presumption that wherever you find money you find brain power. This means that magic is associated and attributed to the financial community. Well, there is no magic.

There is, however, a recurrent tendency to get captured by the speculative mood. That was true in the 1920s and the great crash of 1929. There were speculative episodes in the 1950s and 1960s and of course we had, in the 1980s, the mergers and acquisitions mania, the leverage buyout insanity, the great real estate speculation and the tendency to be carried away by the speculative mood which, as I say, often affects the people, not with the least money, but very often those with the most. It is one of the recurring features of the economy and one that has certainly attracted my attention and to some extent it has attracted my pleasure. There's something – I've said this many times – there's something nice about great tragedy when nothing has been lost but money.

Do you think the future is just another manifestation of this?

Oh no question about it. This manifests itself in many forms. Ever since the Dutch in the seventeenth century went wild on tulips – sombre Dutchmen speculating in tulip bulbs. The South Sea bubble which I suppose has some place in British history still and the recurrent bubbles of the last century. Finally, there has been the Japanese speculation of these last years. This is something which is, I say, part of the system.

It's not just peculiar to America then?

No. It has one central feature which is always worth remembering. It is that a group of people presume to be wise with money and see a price going up or prices going up so they see an opportunity and they buy, against the possibility that it will go up more. And their buying makes it go up more. And that attracts still more buying and forces the price up still further so there is an internal self-generating influence here which is the essence, in one form or another, of the speculative bubble. And then eventually, the supply of new buyers runs out. Eventually the supply of bank credit runs out and it levels off.

41

People decide to get out and then comes the crash. The build up is always somewhat rational in appearance and the crash always very sudden.

Is there anything in a public policy that can be done to meet this or is it endemic in the system and there's nothing we can do about it?

No, I think that the speculative mood is an essential feature of the system and that one of the extraordinary things there is, is that when in the speculative mood people become quite insane about real estate values or stock market values, the person who says that there is an element of insanity there is always criticised. The critic is an inferior sort of person who cannot see the opportunity that exists.

Now we're going to have these cycles and troughs. It's a feature that we're going to have to live with. Is that true also of the real economy, if one might put it like that? We see the financial and monetary economy, but has it an impact on the real economy?

It has an impact on the real economy and has an adverse effect and we should be prepared for that, but I will not surrender quite so readily on the real economy. I would hope that there might come a time when the economy is strong and we would see the opportunity for conservative budget policy, for balancing the budget, for paring down debt. And that we would see that when the economy turns sour, after one of these speculative episodes, this is not the time, not the time to call for restraint, call for cutting down on the budget deficit. That is the time when the government must be a supporting influence. And, as I say, I would hope that we might some day reach the mood, I emphasise this very strongly, when we would see that in a period like the 1980s the government should be a restraining factor. And in a period like the 1990s the government should be a supporting factor. It involves going against the current of the financial mood, but I never sit down to write without hoping that might be possible.

How then do you see the future of the US economy now? What is your vision for the medium term? Is it set fair?

I'm always very cautious about making forecasts because I've discovered over the years that people have an absolutely marvellous memory of your wrong forecasts and they have an extraordinary tendency to forget your right ones. But I would think that there were latent strengths here, latent possibilities that the underemployment equilibrium which we're now suffering will one day be broken. We will see that there's no alternative to government intervention and support such as we're had in the past. The Great Depression was brought to an end by the government intervention of World War II – I don't want a war to end this period of stagnation, I hasten to say that.

The recession of the early 1980s was brought to an end by the strong Keynesian policy of Ronald Reagan and defence build up, which was a strong support for the economy. And I would hope that this might be possible again.

The next time I hope, when the economy is strong, we will then see that is the time of conservative finance as the period of recession is the time for liberal finance.

What about the North American Free Trade Area (NAFTA)?

Oh, I wake up every morning saying to myself well, today I won't engage in any discussion about trade matters; I'll stay with more important questions. We have a broad current in the world for the liberalisation of trade and the internationalisation of trade and I'm all for that. I think that this has been a pacifying influence which carries us away from the enormous tragedies of the first half of this century where one had the awful cost of national conflict.

I support NAFTA for three reasons. First, we should always bear in mind that trade discussions are part of a larger current of media attention. We always see great possible changes and never notice afterwards how little has changed.

Secondly, I have a before and after scenario because I want to see better political relationships between Canada, the United States and Mexico. They're not bad, they're in some ways a model for the world but I want them improved and strengthened and I don't see any great job loss in the United States. I think this has been ridiculously exaggerated; it would be very minor.

And third, the Mexicans are poorer than we are but they are people too, and I would like to see any gesture, any step that we can take to help strengthen the Mexican economy. I don't think that an American can reach conclusions. A good American can reach conclusions only in terms of the United States. I think we are obliged to reach conclusions in terms of a larger community and particularly a larger neighbourly community of Mexico and Canada.

Now, that's an optimistic assessment. Are you naturally an optimistic man or are you a pessimistic man?

Neither, optimism and pessimism both imply some departure from reality. I want to think that I'm intensely realistic.

John Kenneth Galbraith, thank you very much.

Henry Kissinger

What were your first memories of the United States when you arrived?

My first impression was the George Washington Bridge and the skyscrapers. I'd never seen anything like this before but you know it was a pretty overwhelming impression.

Tell me about your education in America. I wonder if I can talk about your time at Harvard. You were an excellent student and then you did graduate work there. What was Harvard like in the 1940s?

When I came to the United States I worked in a shaving-brush factory and went to night school, high school and night college. Then I served in the American army for three and a half years. Harvard was really my first exposure to liberal arts education because when I went to night school and high school it simply was to get a high-school degree. At night college I studied accounting and so my real education started at Harvard.

What kind of atmosphere was it at Harvard, was it very intense?

Yes, you know I was older than the typical undergraduate, I was already twenty-four and it was the postwar atmosphere. The first week we slept in a gymnasium where they had put some beds and then they gradually found places for us. It was more academic than the normal undergraduate experience, since there were fewer extra curricular activities. It was more focused on study. But that was the veterans' generation.

After graduation you went on to do a doctorate and then joined the faculty. It must have been a very stimulating and exciting experience?

Well, to tell you the truth I did not find the faculty at Harvard a very stimulating experience. I think there was a huge gap between the image of themselves and the reality. It was madly competitive, but since the ground rules were elusive, it wasn't clear how you went about competing, so it was a competition in a strange atmosphere and I didn't find it very intellectual either, since people kept guarding their intellectual property. So I didn't find it particularly interesting because as a junior faculty member, everything depended for your advancement on the good will of some senior faculty members. I usually had outside activities so I was less affected than most of the junior faculty. But I do not think of that period as a time of glorious intellectual stimulation. The undergraduate experience was glorious intellectual stimulation, the graduate students were stimulating but not the faculty.

Yet it was a period where you wrote several books, and you established your scholarly career?

Yes, you have a lot of free time at Harvard and you have a great library. But I was not wildly stimulated by Harvard or wildly happy at Harvard. But I have also to be fair in this sense. I was in the field of political science, but I did all my work in history and philosophy. But political science is not a subject, it's like people teaching surgery who've never been in an operating room. They have all these abstract ideas about how politics would work. So, it's an elusive field. In the history department and in the economic department, which had real subjects, the intellectual stimulation was greater, because at least you had a subject matter to which you could refer. Political science attracts people who are drawn into politics, without knowing what politics really is, and that adds to the general ungenerosity of academic life.

What led you into the areas where you established your scholarly reputation?

Well, I've always been interested in history and I became interested in philosophy. I wanted to reflect about the problem of the nature of peace and international order, and so I really, quite at random, picked the period about which I knew absolutely nothing, which was the events surrounding the Congress of Vienna, only because that created a document which more or less lasted a hundred years. That was really what attracted me to it. I had also been interested in Bismarck, because of his impact on the international order, but then I found

47

that in order to write about Bismarck I had to write about the statesmen that had created the international system so ironically, I never wrote about Bismarck; I wrote about the statesmen who had created the Congress of Vienna system.

Did you feel able to apply your analysis for nineteenth century European history to the contemporary world?

I had always been interested in both history and contemporary events. I did not make at first a necessary correlation between the two. But since history is the only experience we have and even if you grant that it does not repeat itself exactly, it is the only way you can train yourself to think about a situation. This came to me gradually over a period of many years. But since I didn't have any fixed plan of going in to government, I didn't need to have an exact correlation worked out.

When did you begin to advise public figures?

When did that start? Fairly early, 1955 I think and I found it interesting.

Well you finally left Harvard to join the Nixon administration. How did you make that decision?

Well, you have to understand I took a very complicated route to becoming a top adviser to Nixon. My career took some amazing turns on the way to joining the Nixon administration. I mean I started my first governmental presidential advisory role with President Kennedy. It was not a direct road to Nixon. My concurrent advisory role was with Governor Nelson Rockefeller who was Nixon's greatest Republican opponent. In fact I had never met Nixon, except for one minute when I shook his hand, until my first interview with him, after he had already been elected, and he was exploring the possibility of my joining the administration. So it is not that when I went to Washington in 1969 I said, at last I've reached what I've always wanted to be. If you had asked me on January 1st 1968 where I would be on January 1st 1969, the last thought I would have had was that I was about to become National Security Adviser to Richard Nixon with whom I had fought all my political life. It was a big wrench to leave Harvard. I didn't have to leave Harvard in one jump because they gave me a two-year leave of absence. So I did not feel it as a big wrench at the time.

So was it a major decision to actually go to Washington?

The big decision was not to go to Washington. The big decision in my mind was whether I could, in good conscience, work for Nixon and retain the friendships that meant something to me. Indeed, when Nixon offered me the job I said to him that I needed a week to consult my friends as to whether I could keep them while working for him. As it happened after two or three days I thought that was not right and called Nixon and told him I was taking the job. So in the end I lost those friends anyway, but on merit, I mean on things that I did, not as a result of my association with Nixon.

What were your first impressions of President Nixon?

Well, he's very shy, and very afraid of being rebuffed and therefore he was very elliptical when he talked to me, so that I didn't know I had been offered a job. I knew he had offered a job, I knew he had offered me something, but I didn't know what and I wasn't quite sure he had offered it to me. I was surprised by how much he knew because I had the typical academic image of him as a gut-fighting, crude politician, which is quite the reverse of the real Nixon. I found him more delicate than I had expected. But, as I said, I didn't know what he had offered and even whether he had offered me anything!

In the White House years did you develop a good working relationship?

Yes, but we never became friends, we are too different. However, I have high regard for him as a statesman, and I've gratitude to him for giving me this opportunity and for giving it generously, for giving me really great scope. It was an excellent working relationship with next to no personal element.

What do you feel were your greatest achievements in those eight years, first as National Security Adviser and then as Secretary of State?

Well, I tried to develop a concept for American foreign policy which is not the way American foreign policy is usually run. Even though we had many critics, in one way or another, the basic design of American foreign policy for the 20 years afterwards and more, was set then. I mean the China initiatives and the Soviet Union initiative. A number of individual things were done, but what we thought was most needed was to take America from the fluctuations between isolationism and over-involvement to a sustainable foreign policy based on concepts that could be understood.

I'm surprised that you didn't mention getting the United States out of Vietnam for which you received the Nobel Peace Prize.

Well, getting America out of Vietnam was essential. It was the precondition for everything else. But by that time American society was so divided, that it was more of a nightmare. It was more surgery than anything else. It was an achievement. I think it was much harder than people understand. I know choices were much more constricted than people understand, or at least than our critics understand.

Those were eight extraordinary turbulent years. How do you look back on the resignation of President Nixon – is it something that leaves you with a great deal of sadness?

I think it was a coup, in the sense that he made huge mistakes, mostly in the nature of petty stupidities. If you ask anyone today to give you a catalogue of what exactly it is that he did that produced all this commotion, it's not so easy to define. Do you see today in the White House a cover up or is it merely an attempt to protect the president? I mean it's the normal reaction for the White House, when the president is attacked, to protect him. Much of what went under the name of Watergate deserves serious condemnation, but it did not require paralysing the government of the United States and changing the President. I said it was a coup, not in the sense it was a planned coup, but there had been an election in 1972, which was fought on ideological issues. So it was one of the few elections that was fought on ideological issues, and the point of view represented by Nixon gained 65 per cent of the vote, yet he could never carry out whatever that mandate represented. So operationally it was a revolution, even if it was a self-inflicted one. I repeat most of the things that went under the name of Watergate were totally wrong. Some of them were absurd, like the so-called enemies list. This was a list of people not to invite to the White House for dinner, and so morons gave it the name of the enemies list. But that's all it was.

How did you cope as Secretary of State while all this was going on?

Well, while all of this was first going on, I was Security Adviser. Thanks to the grace of God or whatever, there was an absolutely total separation in the White House between foreign and domestic policy. So that I was never permitted to participate, thank God, in domestic deliberation. The domestic people never participated in foreign policy deliberation. So even though my office was down the hall from Haldeman's, I had absolutely no knowledge that there was even concern about Watergate, until well into 1973. So it didn't affect me at all, I didn't take it seriously. I thought this was some stupid thing that people were dealing with until well into '73. I mean until about March, late March '73 when it suddenly flew up. I was in a weird position that I had to conduct the foreign policy of the United States with the President, who daily kept losing legitimacy and was increasingly preoccupied with these proceedings. That was the strange situation. But Nixon never conducted foreign policy on political grounds and my only salvation was to try to play it right. In fact from the point of view of domestic support for foreign policy it was not a bad period, because I met once a week with the leaders of the House and the Senate, and they had every interest – I didn't understand this, but precisely because they wanted to get Nixon – to keep something going. So there was great cooperation.

What was your working relationship with President Ford like?

Well, he is a different human bring. My wife says he's the only normal human being we've had as president in 30 years. He's a great American type. I mean Nixon maybe played the statesman, which Ford doesn't claim to be. Ford has tremendous common sense, totally reliable and totally straightforward. What you see is what you get. We did become good friends, and I treasure our personal relationship. He had the reputation of not being very bright, which is totally wrong. He's not all that articulate, but he's very intelligent and he did perform great services for America to keep the ship steady and to see us through a difficult period.

You've not been in public service essentially since the end of the Ford administration but you've observed several administrations. What is your view of the conduct of American foreign policy since you've left office?

Well it depends on the administration. I think Carter had some good people and some good intentions, but he wanted to return to the kind of foreign policy which the period does not really permit. Reagan was a weird phenomenon in the sense that his conceptual apparatus is not extremely highly developed, but he was a good president. Actually I had some tactical problems with his foreign policy.

How was it possible to have no conceptual apparatus and be a good president?

Oh, it's a mystery I have no answer to that question.

How about President Bush?

He was a good professional. He profited at first from the fact that he was the president at the end of an era, and reaped all the successes, and then he suffered from the fact that he was the transition to a new era in which his competences were not as needed as in the previous one.

If you had to advise the Clinton administration on how to conduct itself, what would you tell them?

Talk less and think more.

They don't think enough?

No. I think they are applying by rote.

But has the world changed so fundamentally and is it difficult for the United States to adjust to the new realities?

I think the world has fundamentally changed and it is difficult for the United States to adjust to the new realities, but that's what leadership has to do.

Henry Kissinger, thank you very much.

John Lewis

Congressman Lewis, I wonder if I could start this interview by asking you about your early life and your childhood in the South. What are your most striking memories?

Well, I remember growing up in the South, in rural Alabama, in a very segregated area in the State of Alabama. My father had been a share cropper, a tenant farmer, but in 1944, when I was four years old, and I do remember when I was four, my father had saved $300, and with the $300 he bought 110 acres of land. We moved from the plantation and on this farm we raised a lot of cotton and corn and peanuts, hogs, cows and chickens. We were very poor but somehow and some way we were able to survive and make a living. I grew up in a very large family with six brothers and three sisters. I had a lot of first cousins; on my mother's side I had eight uncles, an aunt, my grandfather and grandmother, great-grandfather and great-grandmother, and so it was a community and a family. There was a great deal of love and a great deal of support. But I saw segregation. I saw racial discrimination. As a young child, when we would visit the little town of Troy, Alabama, or go to Montgomery or some other towns and cities nearby, I saw the signs that said Coloured and White, White man – Coloured man, White women – Coloured women, White waiting room and Coloured waiting room. It was very difficult to be Black and if you stepped out of line, and went to get a drink of water from the wrong fountain, or you took a seat at the wrong place – you could get into real trouble.

Was racial segregation complete? Were there relationships across the colour divide?

Well, from time to time, in a field or in a shop, you could see Blacks and Whites working side by side. In terms of being able to go into a restaurant and get something to eat, or to sit and eat a lunch together, or to share a ride on a bus, or train, or to go to a theatre together, or to attend school together, you did have a racial divide. You knew where to go and where not to go.

What were the attitudes of Black people towards White people; were they hostile and bitter?

55

Now I think for the most part during those years Black people were not hostile toward Whites. There was a sense of peaceful coexistence. I think most Blacks, during those years, resented the system of segregation and racial discrimination, but didn't know how to deal with it. Not until 1955, when Martin Luther King jr. and Rosa Parks led the Montgomery bus boycott. They made people feel, on a mass scale, that they could organise in a dramatic fashion and say no, and protest against a system of segregation and racial discrimination.

Just before we get to the civil rights movement, what was your education like? What memories do you have of primary school and secondary school?

I do remember attending school. My primary education was in a one-room school. Part of it was in a church, the sanctuary of a church, with one teacher. We had the books that had been used by White students. There was very little support from the county or from the state in support of education for people of colour. From the seventh through the twelfth grade I was bussed long distances, for the most part over unpaved roads. We had to pass the White schools to attend segregated schools.

Did your parents encourage you?

My parents did, my mother and my father encouraged me a great deal. My teachers, my minister, they all encouraged me to get the best possible education. They all had limited education. My mother and my father did. They thought education was the passport, that it was the ticket, it was the way out of segregation and racial discrimination.

At what point in your early life did you begin to feel that the system of segregation was just wrong?

During the early teens I guess. I saw it, I resented it, I had tasted the bitter fruits of segregation and racial discrimination. I didn't like the idea that we had to go upstairs to a theatre, that we had to go to the back of a bus. I wanted to do something about it. I knew it was wrong, but something I guess just said to me this is not the way and we don't have to live this way, and there's a better way.

Was there a particular moment or an event that stimulated these set of feelings?

Well, I saw the dual system at my high school – which was called a training school because the high schools for Blacks in rural Alabama were called training schools. So we were being trained to do manual labour and White young people were trained or educated to do something else. I resented it. I saw how Black people were being cheated out of their wages; that people were working from morning to night for starvation wages and it didn't make sense. In the Supreme Court decision of 1954, segregation in public education was held unconstitutional. I was fourteen years old and that inspired me. It gave me hope that I could do something to advance the cause of change in civil rights.

Who were your heroes in your early years?

Well Martin Luther King jr. really emerged as a hero for me, but before Dr King and during those early years in segregated schools in the elementary school, in high school, we had to make scrapbooks of famous and outstanding Black Americans. We were doing what was then called Negro history week, and we now call it African American history month, or Black history month, and so there were people like Booker T. Washington, George Washington Carver, Ralph Bunche, Frederick Douglas and other outstanding African Americans and sports people like Joe Louis and Jackie Robinson. So we collected pictures and wrote stories about these individuals. These were people that we identified with, but later on Martin Luther King jr. emerged. He became my hero and my inspiration – this man inspired me.

And what is your first memory about Martin Luther King jr?

It was the events of the Montgomery Alabama bus boycott in 1955 and '56. This young Black baptist minister, was leading people toward freedom, toward liberation and he was saying some of the things that

I guess I wanted to say and it connected with me, he inspired me. He said this is the way to do it, you can do it. I heard him on the radio, I saw him on television, I read about him in the newspaper and then in 1958, when I was 18 years old, I wrote a letter to him and told him I wanted to attend a little college about 12 miles from my home. That is now Troy State University, and they didn't admit Black students. Dr King wrote me back and sent me a round-trip Greyhound bus ticket and I would never forget it. In the spring of 1958 I boarded the bus and travelled from Troy, Alabama to Montgomery, where I met Dr King for the first time and we became friends. We started working together during my student days, all across the South and all across the country.

So what did you do during your student days and how did you participate in the civil rights group?

Well in the early part of 1959 I started to attend non-violent workshops. So for a whole school year, 1959 to '60, I attended these seminars and workshops in the philosophy and the discipline of non-violence, and got involved in a series of sit-ins, where a group of Black and White college students would go down town and sit at lunch counters and in restaurants and people would come up and put out lighted cigarettes in our hair, or down our backs and pull us off lunch counter stools and beat us. The local police official wouldn't arrest the people that beat us, but they would arrest us, and I went to jail between 1960 and 1966. I was arrested more than 40 times and was beaten during the sit-ins. Later I went on something called a freedom ride, to the segregated areas of public transportation throughout the South, and then I got involved in a series of marches, for the right to vote. At one time in the American South it was very hard and difficult for people of colour to be able to register to vote. You had to pay a poll tax and be able to interpret certain sections of the Constitution. We had to pass the so-called literacy test. We had Black men and women that had postgraduate degrees from some of the best colleges and universities in America. But they flunked the so-called literacy test. They were told they could not read or write well enough and so we organised to gain the vote. I will never forget, in

1965 when the whole effort for the right to vote came to a head, in a little town called Selma, Alabama, in the heart of the Black belt. We were leading this march and it was my day to lead a group of people to the county court house, in Selma. The sheriff of the county was a big man who wore a night stick on one side, gun on the other side and he carried an electric cattle prod in his hand, and he didn't use it on cows he used it on people. He walked up to me and said, 'John Lewis you're an outside agitator, an agitator is the lowest form of humanity', that's what he said to me. I stood there, I looked at him, I looked him straight in the eye, I was almost 25 then, a few pounds lighter, had all of my hair, and I said, 'Sheriff, I may be an agitator, but I'm not an outsider. I grew up only 90 miles from here and we're going to stay here till these people are allowed to register and to vote.' He arrested me and a few other people and took us to jail. A few days later Dr Martin Luther King jr. came to Selma and more than 3000 people were arrested. We filled the jails of Selma. A few miles away a young Black man was shot and killed and because of what happened to him – he was leading the march for the right to vote – we said we would march from Selma to Montgomery. I would never forget it, it was on Sunday March 7 1965, about 625 of us attempted to march through the streets of Selma, Alabama, crossing the Alabama river bridge. It was a silent march, we were walking in twos, we came to the apex of the bridge and then we saw a sea of blue, Alabama State Troopers and a man identified himself and said, 'I'm Major John Cloud of the Alabama State Troopers. I give you three minutes to disburse and go back to your church.' In less than a minute and a half he said 'Troopers advance.' They came toward us, beating us with night sticks, bull whips, trampling us with horses, using tear-gas. That day became known as 'Bloody Sunday.' I was hit and had a concussion and hospitalised for a few days in Selma, Alabama. But the next week, we decided to continue the march. I did march the 50 miles with Dr Martin Luther King jr. from Selma to Montgomery and the Voting Rights Act was passed and signed into law by President Lyndon Johnson.

Hearing that story, the non-violent aspect of it just seems extraordinary. There must have been moments in which you felt so angry that you wanted to respond violently?

I've felt that what was happening to many other people was so wrong. It was hard to believe that people would treat other human beings the way people were treating many of us. But I never had a desire to respond in a violent manner. Many of us during those early years accepted non-violence, not simply as a technique but as a way of life, as a way of living. We came to the conclusion that the means and ends are inseparable. If we were striving to create the beloved community, the open society – if that was our end and if that is our goal – then the methods, the means by which we struggle, must be consistent with the aims. We said, during the early days of the civil rights movements, that we were out to create a truly inter-racial democracy in America. We were out to create a beloved community, to redeem the very soul of America. So if you're going to redeem the soul of America, if you're going to create the beloved community, you've got to use the method and the means of non-violence. You also must believe in it as a way of life, as a way of living.

It must have been difficult sometimes?

It was difficult to see young people beaten, to see the bombing of a church in Birmingham, in 1963 where four young girls were killed while attending Sunday school. It was difficult to see three of your co-workers, two young White men and one Black man, arrested, jailed and then beaten and shot and killed. That is difficult, but somehow and some way you have to believe in the possibility of the human capacity to change.

Martin Luther King jr. must have been a remarkable man; how has the nation suffered from his loss?

Martin Luther King jr. was a remarkable man, he was an unusual, extraordinary human being. This man had the capacity and the ability to give you the feeling that you were somebody. He was a rare, rare human being. He really believed in America. He believed in the potential of human beings to grow and to develop and to change. I think the American community, but more than the American community, the world community has lost a great mind, a leader, a teacher, a philosopher, a preacher, and just a citizen of the world, who really believed that man was evolving to much higher level, where we can live in peace.

Let's take the story on, after the passage of the Civil Rights Act and the Voting Rights Act; what about your career and what did you do in the late sixties and early seventies?

Well, I spent a great deal of time working in the South, for more than seven years in fact, with the voter education project, urging and encouraging minorities to become participants in the democratic process. I got involved in some political campaigns, working for candidates. As a matter of fact I was campaigning with Robert Kennedy, in Indianna when I heard that Dr King had been assassinated on April 4 1968. I thought we could use the political arena as a place to make a greater degree of progress and I felt that Robert Kennedy was in a sense the best hope to advance the cause of civil rights and civil liberties in America. Then Robert Kennedy was assassinated in June of 1968, which was a very dark time. 1968 was not a good year for many of us in the movement. We lost Dr King, we lost Robert Kennedy and these two young men were good friends of mine. Then we witnessed the election of President Nixon, and it was a very dark, dark period. But you don't give up, and I didn't get lost in the sea of despair. I continued and tried to do a few things to help other people, and a lot of people kept encouraging me to turn for office. I recall very well in 1977, when Ambassador Andy Young left the Congress to take the Ambassadorship at the United Nations, I ran for office and I lost that race for Congress. I came to Washington and worked in the Carter Administration, for the Peace Corp and Vista. I went back to Atlanta and became a member of the Atlanta city council and served there for four and a half years. Then I ran for Congress again in 1986, and I won. Today I am serving in the Congress as Deputy Majority Whip in the leadership of the House of Representatives and as a member of the Ways and Means Committee.

If I can just go back to that traumatic year of 1968, was that a watershed? Despite all the difficulties and the beatings and the

hostility of the White establishment, the late 1950s and early 1960s were a time of hope and commitment. Did a light go out in 1968?

Well, I think in 1968 something happened in America, something died in America. It was more than just the death of Robert Kennedy and Martin Luther King jr. Some of that hope, some of that optimism died for many of my friends, and many other people who had struggled with me. Some literally dropped out, some of them just gave up, and have not been able to return to the process, to political participation. It was a very dark hour, it was a very dark year and I'm not so sure whether we, as a people and as a nation, have dealt with 1968. I think many of us say, from time to time, if it hadn't been for 1968, if Martin Luther King jr. had lived, if Robert Kennedy had lived, and been elected President of the United States, maybe our nation, maybe our world, would be altogether different.

What gave you the commitment to continue in public service? Was it a belief that somehow you could make a difference?

I think what kept me going was a sense of hope. You have to believe that things will get better, that you sort of make up your mind that you will not get lost, and be sidetracked. You accept the idea that there maybe some disappointments, some setbacks here and there, maybe some interruptions, but you cannot give up, and I think some place along the way during the mid to late sixties I came to the conclusion that I'll struggle, that I'll fight. It's not for just one day or one week, or one month or one year or one lifetime; you have to continue to do what you can, while you live and say to a future generation that you also must become a participant in this continuing effort to make our society something different, something better.

As you reflect back on your career and public life, has the position and the circumstances of Black Americans improved considerably?

I think the conditions, the circumstances, of Black Americans have changed and have improved a great deal. The signs that I saw when I was growing up, those simple signs that said, White waiting, Coloured waiting, White man, Coloured man, White women, Coloured women, those signs are gone and they will not return, they are gone forever and the generation yet unborn will not see those signs in America. The young people who have grown up today will not see those signs. But racism still exists and it must be removed. But the element of fear, that was so widespread all across the South, during the fifties and the sixties, that element of fear, is gone. People can stay in the same hotel, ride together in the same taxi cab, you can sit where you want on a bus or a train. You can buy a house where you like, you can own a business. So you do see all across the South, pockets of what I would like to call integration, pockets of people building and working together. So, life is different. In 1965 there were less than 50 Black elected officials in 11 southern states of confederacy from Virginia to Texas. Today, there are more than 6000, in these 11 states. We didn't have any Black members in the Congress, from the Deep South, during the sixties. Almost every southern state, except for one, has at least one Black member of the Congress. So we have come a distance, we have made a great deal of progress, but we still have a distance to go before we create the beloved community, before we create a truly inter-racial democracy in America. But we're on our way, and there won't be any turning back.

For that generation of remarkable people who embraced non-violence does the existence of such bitterness and hostility and violence in the Black community distress you?

I'm very distressed and deeply concerned about so many things that I see happening today in the Black community. I think maybe we have not played the role that we should have played. We have not carried out the mission that we should have performed in terms of educating this generation of young people to the importance of holding on to something like the philosophy and the discipline of non-violence. Many young people today in our communities don't have a sense of contemporary history. They need to know how these changes came about. So, what we need now, I think more than anything, is to teach, to educate, but also we must instill in young people, especially young Blacks, but all young people in America, a sense of values. I say over and over, to the young people that I come in contact with, that I went to jail a few times, but not for fighting, not for using drugs, not for using a gun, but for trying to make our country different, better, for trying to make us live up to the Constitution, to the Declaration of Independence, to the Bill of Rights, and what we need now in America more than anything, I think, is a revolution of values, a revolution of ideas, not a revolution in the streets. But a revolution in the very spirit and the hearts of American people.

What about yourself, what are your own goals? You're still a young man and still have a career ahead of you. Where do you see yourself going?

Well, I would like to continue to serve here in the House of Representatives, to serve in the Congress, make a contribution, by helping the people in the state of Georgia and the people of this nation and people around the world. I wouldn't rule out the possibility one day of maybe seeking the higher office, of maybe a Senate seat in Georgia, or some other position in the State of Georgia. But as right now, for the next few months and few years, I think my role is to continue to speak out against violence and to speak for the philosophy and the discipline of non-violence and try to spend a great deal of my time with young people in my own district. I go back every weekend and I spend time going from school to school reaching people while they are very young and discussing the philosophy and the discipline of non-violence. Saying to young people there is a better way, there is a different way.

A final question Congressman. You've lived a life in difficult and turbulent times and it appears to me that you've always had a positive and hopeful view of the future; is that something you continue to retain?

I believe that I'm very hopeful and very optimistic about the future, and I think that the only way to survive and be at peace with yourself, is to believe that things are going to get better. But they're not going to get better just by saying they're going to get better. You believe it and then you try to set things in motion; you have to create the climate, create the environment. I believe that. But in doing so there are certain principles that I believe are non-negotiable, and one of those is my deep and abiding faith and belief in the dignity of human kind, the dignity of man. I happen to believe that the human personality is something very special and very sacred and that you do not destroy it, you do not abuse it and that's why I accept the philosophy and the discipline of non-violence as a way of life, as a way of living. I believe in non-violence. You have to have a sense of hope because the two go hand in hand.

Congressman John Lewis, thank you very much.

Walter Mosley

Walter Mosley, can I start this conversation by asking you what does it feel like to be President Clinton's favourite novelist?

I am happy that President Clinton likes my books. I'm happy that he has read them. I am happy that he talks about them. It's a good thing and it also means something in America. To have a White male president read is a big thing, but also to read a Black American male writer is kind of stunning!

Tell me about how you got into writing thriller fiction.

I came to it in a funny way. I'm an eclectic reader, I read everything, I enjoy a good writer, and I have read a lot of crime fiction, American crime fiction. When I started writing I wasn't writing crime fiction, I was writing about Black people in America. And one of the problems about being a Black male writer in America is that people keep wondering 'who's going to read this?' They are very much into these niche markets. If you're an Irish American writer, you're writing for Irish American. But a Black American male writer? Because some of the Black American males don't read, they didn't know what to do with my work. And so when I came back to it I said, 'well, I'll make this one into a mystery'. It was just because I enjoyed writing, I was playing with it. And it started to sell, so I kept on.

So prior to writing the first novel, what had you been doing?

I'd been a computer programmer for 15 years, and a variety of other things. I'd been a caterer for a while, I was a porter; I did all kinds of things.

And the first novel was your first attempt at writing fiction?

No. The first novel I wrote was about the same characters, Easy Rawlings and Raymond Mouse Alexander, as 18-year-olds in the Deep South. It was a psychological novel, two poor young basically uneducated Black men thinking about their fathers. One, Easy, whose father had abandoned him when he was a child, is trying to remember him and trying to understand and forgive him for that. And

67

Mouse wanted to find his stepfather and kill him, just because he hated him. So it was this strange kind of journey that both men were on. But nobody wanted to publish that because it was about two young Black men in the Deep South. They said 'who would wanna read about that?'

From where do you derive the experience for writing the Easy Rawlings novels?

I don't know. I guess it's from a variety of places. It's from the stories that I've heard from my family, my father especially, and other people around. Not just the stories themselves but also the way the stories were told. A lot of things about all our acting comes from the unconscious, so I'll just start writing and things will come out of me, things that I don't quite know what they are or where they come from, and then I have to try to put them in place inside the fiction.

What about the location and the time period? Why did you choose those?

Well, I think that's a very important time. 1948 in Los Angeles in California is right after the war. It's when people started to flood into Southern California, and it's when Black people in the Deep South realised that they didn't have to live the kind of lives they were living in the Deep South. They could get away from that, they could go get a good job and buy property and live with some measure of equality. So that was the beginning of a period of transition and hope that didn't quite work out. I want to provide a map through the years of how it didn't.

Were you brought up in Los Angeles?

Yes, I was born there in 1952, and lived there until about 1970.

So did you have to do a great deal of research about the period in those postwar years?

No, I haven't done a great deal of research. I do some, but you know, the idea of the novel as a historical tool is a tool of language. It's less what happened and more how people experienced what happened. How people talk, how people move from place to place, how they relate to each other, what they think about their world and the future. And so most of my work is about that which I know. I do some research, and some of this research is horrible. I went to Los Angeles recently and I was reading old newspapers. It was so depressing, I got a headache. I read the *Los Angeles Times* for a two-week period. One Black person was talked about, Duke Ellington who happened to be playing at the Third Monterey Jazz Festival. I read also the Black newspaper for the whole month of September. Martin Luther King was mentioned once; Malcolm X, not at all. It was just horrible.

How much of you is invested in the character of Easy Rawlings?

That's very hard to say. You know, I'm not a confessional writer. So the stories I'm telling are not really stories about my life. I think Easy reflects my questions about right and wrong. This is the big thing, I think, about Easy's character. He's always trying to figure out what's right and wrong, because he's on the wrong side, because the law doesn't really apply to him unless it's going to put him in jail – that's when he thinks about right and wrong. He also has to think about his own best interests. And these are questions that I've asked myself lots. So he shares a lot of my thoughts, but I've not got Easy's personality.

So how do you get into somebody like that?

This is a very difficult question to ask. I know a lot of people have answers for these things. They seem to understand where their characters come from and what their characters are thinking and why they think it. I don't really know at all. I start writing about Easy. Easy falls in love with a woman. Well, why does he fall in love with her? He doesn't know that, I mean how am I going to know it? I start to write and I feel the voice coming out of me, I know that that's right and I just keep on working.

Can I take you back to the Los Angeles of the postwar period? Do you think that was a particularly important location for Black Americans just after the war?

Oh, it was very important because it was a moment that was perfect for Black people. Black men had just come back from the war and saw themselves in a different way. The war had just happened and America had proven that it was the boss of the world for the next 20 years. There was an incredible amount of money, and you had a city that didn't exist before, so you didn't have people who were already in power, like maybe the Irish as electricians and the Polish as the plumbers. They needed electricians and plumbers and painters, and if you could do the work they would hire you. So there was a kind of an economic integration. They said, 'Well, we've got some painters,' they said, 'Well, you know we got a Jew, we got a couple of Blacks, we got a Mexican, we got some Japanese', and that was just the way it was. You can still see that integration in the labour force in Los Angeles. So you had a situation which was perfect for Black people to start to develop lives better than those they had experienced for the previous three centuries.

And how does Easy Rawlings fit into this city in 1948?

He doesn't fit very well because he's too ambitious. Like I said, you could come in and you could be a janitor or a painter, you could be a plumber, but if you wanted to be an entrepreneur, if you wanted to be a real-estate mogul, if you wanted to make a life in which you're important, now this was a problem.

What about Easy's attitudes towards White people, and authority generally?

I think that Easy really wants to pay attention to authority, but he also wants to be part of that authority. He wants to be a person that people come to for advice and he wants them to listen to him. White people don't listen to him; White people think that he's nothing, and less than nothing, that he's stupid because of the way he looks, because of the colour of his skin. This drives Easy crazy. People disrespect him all the time, and he just has to ignore it, but every time they do it, there's another bit of weight on him, another pressure.

Who has been a formative influence in your writing in crime fiction? Is it people like Raymond Chandler, Dashiel Hammet and Chester Himes?

Actually, I didn't start reading Chester Himes until after I wrote *The Devil in a Blue Dress*. There's three people who influenced me. There's Chandler and Hammet, as you say. And they kind of influenced the heart of my fiction, where it comes from. Ross MacDonald influenced how I answer questions because Ross MacDonald asks psychological questions, and my books are very psychological. It's a very hard thing to do, to keep a story rolling along.

Do you see Easy Rawlings in that tradition of Macdonald's Lew Archer and Chandler's Philip Marlowe, as a kind of white knight?

I see him as coming out of it and also as a critical response to it. You see, the earlier gumshoes who I like, they are White men of European descent who have no mother, no father, no sister, no brother, no property, no job. So they don't have anything that would make them responsible to the world. Easy isn't like that. Easy has a wife, or, at least an ex-wife, he has children, he has friends, he has property, he has things that make him have to do things in the world.

The old-time, hard-boiled detective has no mother, father, sister, brother, child, job, property. So when he gets arrested, if he thinks there's something wrong, he'll just sit there and say, 'Oh, I'll just stay here, you know.' And they say, 'Well, we'll kill you.' He says, 'I don't care, kill me.' And he can stand up for his rights because he's not responsible to anyone. Easy, on the other hand, has children, he has property, he has friends. He has a child and an ex-wife. So when he goes to jail, for instance, in my new book, he's in jail, the first thing that he wants to do in jail is get out because his kids are at home. He has to go feed them. And so this is a step beyond the earlier fiction. I think the earlier fiction was necessary, but Easy answers moral questions by being implicated in the world, rather than being perfect.

I was struck by your earlier remark that people didn't recognise Easy as an intelligent man of the world, and yet here he is, a man of really quite considerable property, but he conceals it, doesn't he? Why?

Because he learned when he lived in the Deep South that anything you had, could be taken away from you, and there was no recourse. White people could take it from you. Black people could take it from you. If you told somebody you had some money, they were gonna come in and they were gonna get that money away from you. So he keeps everything a secret, even when he doesn't have to. And that's interesting. One of the interesting things about racism is that it's not so much how it comes from the outside, you can deal with that, but the way it comes from the inside, that's really the problem. In the film *Fires in a Mirror*, Conrad Muhammed says that when he starts to talk about the fact that they did terrible things to us as slaves, but the worst thing they did was take away our knowledge of ourselves, so we could never come back to who we are, we could never recover. That's one of Easy's problems.

And is that what distinguishes Easy from Marlowe or Archer, the fact of being Black? Is that the point of distinction?

Well, I think that is one of the major ones. I think that you could also write about a White detective who faces the same kind of issues as Easy, and some people have. Charles Willerford does. Charles Willerford writes about real people. But certainly that's another dimension, and it's hard for a White man and a White world to recognise the racial dimension.

I wonder if you could tell me a little bit about yourself, about growing up in Los Angeles. You said you were born in the early fifties. What was Los Angeles like in the early fifties?

You know, it was a wonderful place in a lot of ways. There was lots of hope, there was lots of opportunity. People came from the South so they were pretty conservative, and believed in, you know, morality and religion and education. It was kind of a wonderful place. And because I was raised in a Black community there was very little racism, because everybody was Black so it was very hard to be racist against anybody. Later on, when I moved to an integrated community, the problems started to happen because of the conflicts between White and Black. LA was a real hope, a real place of possibility. It isn't any longer, but it used to be.

I'm struck by that, both the statements that LA was a place of possibility and it isn't any longer. What kind of possibilities and why have those possibilities come to an end?

Well, it was possible for people who never had anything to make something of themselves and of their lives. People in Los Angeles could work as much as they wanted when I was a kid. If you had one job and you worked really hard doing that, if you didn't have enough money you got another job, to work hard doing that. And if that didn't work you could work on the weekends too. You could make money, you could buy property, you could be a real person in the world, or even a force in the world. But you know, America has changed on the whole. You know, when I was a kid, America owned the world, basically. We took the profits from South America and Asia and Africa. We were paternalistic towards Europe. We had everything, and so even poor people could make money in America when I was a kid. That's not true any more, that's a kind of Marxist argument, you know. The people on the edge, they can't work any more. They don't have a job any more, so I think that's really the major problem. It's not internal, it's not a racist issue, it's more a class issue.

And these possibilities in the fifties and sixties were available to Black people as well?

Oh yeah, sure, you could work. You see, you're talking about people who were coming from places where all they could do was sweep up after the White man. As a guy says in one of my books, 'All I could do was sweep up after the White man, and I had to bring my own broom.' And that's the kind of jobs you had so you didn't get paid anything and you couldn't live in a good neighbourhood. But in Los Angeles, you could do any kind of job, and you could rise. You couldn't become a lawyer, I mean it was unlikely you're gonna become a lawyer or a doctor, but you could become a carpenter or a plumber or electrician. You could belong to a union, you could make good money. You could have a nice house in a neighbourhood. You could live a pretty good life.

But your background wasn't prototypically Black. You're partly Jewish?

Right, my mother.

And how did that affect your life?

It's hard to say. The more I talk about things, the more I begin to realise that it's hard to understand where you are and where you've come from, because I don't know where I might have been. I think that certain aspects of life were open to me because of the Jewish side of my family. That certain ways of talking, of discourse, of seeing oneself in the world were available to me that might not have been available to people that I went to school with for instance. But I have a lot of friends who are Black who lived in the same neighbourhoods that I did, from when I was a child until I grew up, who are very similar to me and see the world a lot in the same ways. So it's really hard to say, and I try so much not to define myself as being different, because if you start to define yourself as being different, in a way you've been defeated by the external forces.

An American identity is a very complicated business. There is an enormous complexity about it. Is there any tension between the Black and Jewish elements of your heritage?

You mean conflict in me? Ah, no. I think that a lot of that has to do with the fact that I accept myself and my parents accepted themselves. They lived together until my father died at the beginning of this year. I loved who they were and so I love who I am.

We've talked about the fact that Easy Rawlings is Black and a powerful theme of race runs through all your books. Are there any Jewish themes evident in the books?

There are, but I think that they are minor themes. And I think that reflects my experience in America. Because, you see, if you're Black in America, if you have just a tiny little bit of Black in you, that means you're Black, period. There's no question about it. Black is Black and White is White and these two things don't come together. And, you know, some people mistake the idea. They think that being White and being Jewish you're somehow someone who I don't agree with. But of course I have a Jewish background. In *A Red Death*, for instance, the book in which I talk the most about Jewish people, I have a union organiser who was a Communist in Poland, fought against the Germans and came to America and started organising here. And he identifies with Black people because he'd seen people burned and hung and who were forced to live in ghettos. He's seen people killed because of their race, because being Jewish was a race. So he identifies with Black people in America. In my first book, Easy talks about having liberated a concentration camp, and his relation to the people coming out of the camps. There are also two people, two Jewish men, both of whom were in the camps, and they run a liquor store in the Black community which was a very common thing. One was stealing from the other, you know!

Was your mother religious?

No. My mother wasn't religious. Of course I don't think most Jews in America are religious. It's more of a cultural thing. How significant was it? It's hard to say. I loved my family, my Uncle Chaim and my Aunt Fanny, my cousin Lily, who would make me gefilte fish and chicken soup. I liked these people, I liked going to their houses, I like to hang out with them, they were fun. So I loved them as people. It's hard to come to some sort of cultural understanding of what kind of impact that had on me. That seems to be a mistake, a lot of people in America are looking for it [cultural understanding], you know, when they're looking for their ethnicity. They're looking for something that goes unspoken in life. Your life with other people is a question of how you feel about them, how you feel about yourself, and what your language is like, and how you like telling stories, not so much what the social or cultural meaning is.

Does any of this affect Easy in any way?

Does my Jewish background affect Easy? I am sure it does, but I couldn't tell you how.

Is it a source of great pain to you that a bitter conflict appears to have built up between Jews and Blacks over the last 10 to 15 years?

Again, this seems to be an economic issue. A funny one. Because in America, media is knowledge. And underneath that media is money. And so if you have a newspaper, you need a headline that's going to make people buy the newspaper. And so if you see a conflict between a Black person and a Jewish person, you're gonna put that on the headline because people will buy the newspaper. And sooner or later people are going to begin to believe that Jews and Blacks don't like each other, and they're in conflict, and of course there's a lot of Black anti-Semites and there is a lot of hatred from Jews towards Blacks, or at least the fear. But a lot of Blacks and Jews get along perfectly well. I know this because I exist. I know this also because I know Black people and Jews who get along and who work together, who like each other, who have fun in their lives. There is a bitter conflict in America but it's only part of a much larger social reality. It's not like Bosnia. I feel unhappy when I see conflicts that I know could be resolved, that don't need to exist. But I don't feel despair, because I see other things.

Do you think part of the reason for the publicity about this conflict is that historically Jews and Blacks have got on very well and therefore a breakdown between the communities is all the more striking and all the more newsworthy?

I think that the breakdown between the two communities has a lot to do with this concept of ethnicity, of defining yourself beyond some kind of human categories. Black people, of course, have been trying very hard in America to define themselves, to have an identity, to be taken seriously, at least by themselves. And Jews, on the other hand, some have returned to religion and a lot to the political reality of Israel. And a lot have forgotten what it was like not to be White. A lot of them don't realise that they aren't the White people they think that they are.

It appears that Jews seem to be particularly hurt by the anti-Semitism expressed by someone like Louis Farrakhan.

Because there's been an attempt on the part of many Jewish Americans to support Black political movements. When somebody in the Black community acts in what seems like an anti-Semitic way, they feel that they've been kind of slapped in the face by somebody that they've been helping. But at the same time there's a response from the Black community, due to a very paternal kind of attitude of Jews towards Black people. For instance, Jewish organisations and individuals saying, well I can't support you unless you publicly denounce Farrakhan, or Jesse Jackson, or whoever. And this becomes a problem because you know what you're doing is you're trying to get into somebody's business. If you wanted to help, you would help, but if you didn't want to help, you'd stay out. Of course, when you're giving somebody money, you have a right to ask them for things. It's like a family, it's like a little family feud, you know. It's a very hard thing to figure out.

And do you feel this personally as it were, or do you somehow stand apart from it? When these divisions blow up, is it particularly painful for you?

I really don't like it. But I have to keep going back to the fact that there are a lot of people who know how to get along. I think most people know how to get along, so I don't feel terribly unhappy. I do feel unhappy when I see Black people who deny that there was ever a Holocaust, who have a particular disdain for Jews above other White people. But I feel kind of hopeful. My experience is that people do get along, so I don't feel too bad about it.

How about you, where do you go from here? You're writing your fourth Easy Rawlings novel. Where do you see the future?

Well, I'm going to write a few more Easy Rawlins novels. *Black Betty* is the book I'm working on right now. I'm going to write a book about Robert Johnson called *R.L.'s Dream*. It's a book in which Robert Johnson is the negative space. I talk about a fictional blues character who once played blues in the delta with Robert Johnson. I'm going to keep on writing and try to be a better writer. It becomes harder and harder as you go along, but it's a kind of simple path for me right now.

I understand Holywood beckons.

Ah yes. They're supposed to be making a movie. Maybe they will, who knows. Jonathon Demme is the executive producer, Carl Franklin is the director and Denzil Washington is starring in *Devil in a Blue Dress*. Carl Franklin wrote the screenplay, and hopefully it will be a wonderful movie.

Do you have any role to play in the making of the movie?

I'm called the associate producer. That means that Carl Franklin asks me questions and I try my best to answer him.

Does it please you that it's going on to the big screen?

That's a good question. I don't know yet. I have to wait until I see it there. Hollywood is a funny place. I like to work with it, I like it that they want to make my film because you could make money on it. But, you know, I'm in love with the novel. It seems to me that the place where real information is still gathered in this world is in the novel. And so I'm more excited about the fact that my books get printed.

Do you think you will ever write a contemporary novel?

Yes, definitely. There's a novel that I want to write, a coming-of-age novel, about a young Black man who is living in Harlem with this alcoholic father, his schizophrenic mother and his great-grandfather, who lives in a room. And this young man is a computer programmer-type, down on Wall Street, and his day is split between Wall Street and his experience there and Harlem and his experience there, and how he has to bring these things together. It seems to me like an interesting coming-of-age novel. I like some coming-of-age novels, but there's usually a young White male, upper middle-class person who is obsessed sexually. Everybody's obsessed sexually, it doesn't seem to be much of an issue that there are all these other people who are experiencing this, yet it never gets out there into the public. That's something I really would want to do.

Do you feel optimistic about race relations in the United States?

Well, there's never been racial harmony in the United States. I don't know about the rest of the world. I assume it hasn't been there either. But in the United States, there has never been racial harmony and things haven't changed very much. They vacillate, they go back and forth, but they haven't changed very much. And when I think about that, I think about the experience of the Jews in Europe. There's a thousand years of anti-Semitism in Europe. Sometimes they weren't bad, and sometimes they were terrible, culminating in the Holocaust. To think things are getting better is a mistake. To try to keep them from getting worse, is more the right attitude, it seems to me.

The Jewish experience in America has been pretty good, hasn't it?

Jewish experience in Germany was pretty good on the whole. Most of the history of Jews in Germany was great. So yes, but you have to take that with a grain of salt, or a sense of history.

If Easy Rawlins was in LA in 1993, would he . . .

He will be.

He will be?

He will be, he's going to be old, he's going to be a detective, in at least 1991 anyway. He'll be very different. One of the things that I try to do to books is keep the character interesting by aging him, so he gets older and older and he has different experiences. When a person comes up to the young Easy Rawlins in 1948, when Easy is twenty-eight, and says that they are afraid of death, Easy may empathise with him, but not from the inside. But when Easy's in his mid-seventies and someone says 'I'm afraid of death', it'll have a whole other meaning to Easy. So I really want to write about LA in the 1990s, from Easy's point of view. I'm not sure what it'll be yet, I don't know what he'll think, but we'll see.

A final question. What ambitions do you have left?

I'm getting pretty sure that I'm a writer. And so the idea is to become as good a writer as I can be. That, right now, is an ambition of mine, and it's the only real burning ambition of mine. I love to write, and I love great fiction, and I want to bring my work to higher and higher levels.

Walter Mosley, thank you very much

Arthur Schlesinger

You've had a long and distinguished record as an academic and indeed in public life. What have been the highlights of your career?

Probably the highlight of my career was my second book which came out in 1946 *The Age of Jackson*, and it's been downhill ever since then. But my base has always been in the university and in academic life, but I've always had a fascination with politics. I have been involved in the margin of politics for a time. I suppose the most exhilarating time of my life was when I was a special assistant to President John Kennedy in the White House during the early 1960s.

Well why don't we talk a little about that; what was so exhilarating?

Well for a historian to have the opportunity to watch history being made and be a witness and indeed, to some extent, a participant in the making of history, is obviously a great experience. I think one gets a much greater sense of the extent to which history is more a matter of improvisation, accident, chance, than it is of planning. I think historians have a tendency to tidy up the past in retrospect. They see a pattern where in fact it was more an accumulation of possibilities often brought about by people who lacked the proper information or who were under too much pressure, or whatever. So I think you have a more accurate sense of the way, at least in the field of public policy, history is made, if you've been there yourself. Gibbon, who was a part-time soldier, wrote in his autobiography, that being a Captain of the Hampshire Grenadiers was not entirely useless to the historian of the Roman Empire.

I know in the immediate aftermath of the assassination you started writing A Thousand Days. At that time you clearly had a very positive view of the Kennedy administration. Thirty years on have you modified that view?

Yes, I've modified that view in some respect and I wrote a second book. *A Thousand Days* was essentially a memoir of my own experience. I wrote a second book about Robert Kennedy, which was a much more detached attempt at taking, among other things, a fresh look at some of the issues that arose in the Kennedy years. I think, for example, that the administration overreacted to a very truculent speech that Kruschev gave in Moscow in 1961, a fortnight before Kennedy's inauguration. I think Kennedy and the rest of us overreacted to that speech, and I think that launched an unnecessary arms build-up in the United States that forced the Russians to do likewise. In the longer run though, that process may well have hastened the collapse of the Soviet economy, particularly as it was compounded by President Reagan in the 1980s.

Do you feel on balance that you have retained your admiration for Kennedy?

Oh yes. I think the current effort to deprecate the accomplishments of that administration is quite wrong. I think he led the way. We now know that the Cuban missile crisis in 1962 was even more dangerous than we supposed at the time. I was in Havana a few years ago with Castro and one of the top Soviet generals and others, including Bob MacNamara, Kennedy's Secretary of Defence, when the general told us that nuclear warheads were in Cuba in 1962. We had never been clear on this at the time. We were also told that the Soviet command in Cuba had been delegated the authority to retaliate against an American invasion by the use of tactical nuclear weapons, whose existence in Cuba we had never suspected. So, for all that, I think he handled that very well. But then Kennedy moved on to the American University speech and the Test Ban Treaty. I think had Kennedy lived, Kruschev might have survived a little longer and together I think they would have made much more progress toward *détente*.

It is interesting, speaking with you, because you are the biographer of another very prominent Democratic President, Franklin Roosevelt. How does Kennedy compare with Roosevelt?

Well Kennedy never had the same opportunity. I mean he was only President for a thousand days or so, Roosevelt was elected President four times. And Roosevelt moreover had major crises to deal with. He had the worst depression in our history and the worst war in our history. These crises both challenged and tested the metal of a President but they also gave him more opportunity because if a crisis is perceived and accepted, and the crises of depression and war are very palpable crises, this widens the range of possibilities for possible actions for a president.

And in your view does Roosevelt continue to remain one of the greatest Presidents?

Oh yes, I think, even Republicans now concede that. And the occasional polls taken amongst American historians and political scientists, he invariably comes out with Washington and Lincoln as one of our three greatest Presidents.

You've got a unique perspective on the twentieth century; is it your view that something has gone awry in the United States in these last few decades as the twentieth century comes to an end?

Well, I don't know whether it's unique to the United States. There appears to be a collapse of political leadership everywhere in the world, whether it's an illusion or not. When I grew up in the 1930s you had these colossal figures everywhere you looked – Roosevelt and Churchill, Stalin and Hitler and Mussolini. Later on there was Mao and de Gaulle and so on. There doesn't seem to be leadership of that character today, whether it's an optical illusion or not, but as I look around the world, practically every political leader in any part of the world is fighting for his life or her life at this point. So I think the US is in trouble, but I don't think it's in basic trouble. There is a school of thought talking about decline; well there's been a relative decline in America's influence in the world. At the end of the Second World War we had galvanised American industrial capacity and at the same time America had been very little damaged by the war. So we enjoyed a kind of artificial economic pre-eminence, which was bound to come to an end as other countries began to restore their own economies. And that has happened. And of course both Japan and Germany having a great advantage in the 1940s, '50s and '60s of being denied defence spending, were able to forge ahead in civilian technologies of various sorts. But even Japan and Germany are having their economic troubles today for various reasons, so I think the United States basically has the scientific and technological dynamism, the varied and resourceful population, the robust national ideals and so on to pull itself together.

As a foreign observer, recent American political leaders, I'm thinking particularly of Presidents Carter, Reagan and Bush, have not been enormously impressive. Do you have some sympathy with this view?

I totally agree with it. They are not terribly impressive to a lot of Americans. In fact, I think the last really effective President was Lynden Johnson, and Johnson was a kind of a tragedy, in a way, because what he was good at and what he understood and was knowledgeable about, was domestic policy. In domestic policy he knew where he was going, but in foreign policy his views were rigid and simplistic. And the sadness of his administration was, he sacrificed domestic policy in which he was an expert, to the foreign policy of Vietnam, in which he was misled.

Can I just pick up on your remarks about the future of the United States? You said that you had confidence about the future because the United States had the right kind of cultural mix and cultural values. I know this is an issue of some concern to you. Can we explore this because I know you've put pen to paper and articulated your concerns about the assertion of individual cultures within the United States?

Yes, I think that you have to see the problem against a large historical global context. The twentieth century was essentially a century of a warfare between ideologies. Democracy versus fascism in the first half of the century, democracy versus communism in the second half. This was a contest which liberal democracy won. Fascism perishing with a bang, communism with a whimper, but the cessation or the suspension of ideological warfare does not, as some say, mean the end of history. I think what happens is one set of hatred replaces another, and very deep seated ethnic, national, religious and linguistic antagonisms which were repressed during the Cold War, are now bursting forth all over the world. What's happening in Yugoslavia is just a murderous portent of the future. If the twentieth century saw the warfare of ideologies, the twenty-first century is going to see the warfare of ethnicities. At least it's going to begin that way.

The US is the only large multi-ethnic state that has more or less held together for a couple of centuries. I think it's worthwhile understanding why it has held together, I mean even Canada is on the verge of break-up over ethnic linguistic differences. The reason the US has succeeded to the extent that it has, has been that from the beginning, the notion of an American identity has absorbed and transcended all the various group identities of group cultures that came to these shores. America has been immeasurably enriched by these various subcultures that have come here and it's been changed. The American identity is constantly in the making and has been changed by the newcomers. Nonetheless, the thing has worked, because the newcomers accept their being American as their prime identity. And America has been a country of individuals not of groups. The Constitution is written for individuals not for groups. What has happened in recent years, for a variety of reasons, has been an eruption of a cult of ethnicity. A fellow named Michael Novak wrote a book 25 years ago called *The Rise of the Unmeltable Ethnics*, about ethnics who resisted the melting pot, and he argued that groups should define the character of American life rather than individuals. Although Novak was writing in the interests of East Europeans, the general viewpoint was taken up very vigorously by the non-White minorities, or rather by the self-appointed spokesman from these minorities. So you've had, in recent years, this tendency to see America as a federation of groups, various distinct and immutable ethnic groups, rather than a nation of individuals. Multiculturalism depends on what you mean by it. When multiculturalism means teaching our kids about other continents, other cultures, other creeds, other colours, obviously it's fine, because it means you teach American history, giving new credit to the achievements of the non-Anglo minorities in this country. Well, that's long overdue. If it means teaching history from a variety of viewpoints, the arrival of Columbus from the viewpoint of those who met him as well as from the viewpoint of those who sent him, that's excellent too. But when multiculturalism means that the aim of education should be to promote and perpetuate separate ethnic and racial communities, that seems to be a more disturbing development. To some degree there's been an effort, particularly in public schools, to try to use those schools, which historically have been the great agency of converting newcomers into Americans, to promote and reinforce separate cultures, which seems to be troubling.

Why do you think this has happened to groups rather than individuals and why has the notion of separatism taken hold?

Well, I think it is important to distinguish between the self-appointed spokespersons for these groups. Gunnar Myrdal of Sweden wrote *The American Dilemma*, the best book about our race problem, half a century ago. He came back to the United States in the 1970s and he was struck by this phenomenon of what he called romantic ideologues who did not, in his view, represent the rank and file of the minorities for which they claimed to speak. And that's really essentially the case. I think that Michael Novak was an East European example and then many people have followed, speaking for the Blacks, for the Hispanics, for the Asian Americans and so on. Some of them, because they really honestly cherish a culture, others because they want to preserve or develop a constituency. But I think there's also a perfectly legitimate argument for ethnic groups cherishing their traditions, their costumes, their festivals, their parades and their cuisines. This enriches the texture of American life, and there's conflict between that and a sense of an overriding American identity. I think in spite of what the ideologues say, most Blacks wanted to join the mainstream. Recent polls of Hispanics show that most of them want to learn English; they don't want to remain in a Spanish-speaking ghetto. So you have, I think, the appeal of the mainstream which is far more potent than the separatist appeals of the ideologues. I believe the real cause of the trouble lies in the complacent White majority in this country, because assimilation and integration is a two-way street; not only must the minorities wish it, but the majority, the people who think they own America, must be prepared to welcome those who wish to join America. I think America historically has been a racist country; racist for most of our existence, in its laws and its institutions. Racism has been the great scandal of American history and one of the still crippling diseases of American society. It's White racism that gives the romantic ideologues their opportunity to make their appeals, but I think the rank and file of all the minorities would like nothing better than to be able to join the mainstream.

Can an American identity be emotionally, and I suppose psychologically, satisfying to this extraordinarily diverse population?

Oh I think so, and I tell you what gives me the greatest confidence is the most telling statistic, the rates of intermarriage. Intermarriage across ethnic lines, intermarriage across religious lines and increasingly intermarriage across racial lines. So, though I wrote a booked called *The Disuniting of America*, I think it's a tendency about which people must be much more aware than they are. I think the dangers of ideological multiculturalism must be understood, but I think the best guarantee against the disuniting of America is sex and love. People are going to intermarry, and once they intermarry then most Americans are, and will continue to be, of mixed ethnic ancestry, therefore they won't identify with one or other ethnic community. They see themselves primarily as Americans so that is the basis of my long-term optimism.

Has this ideological multiculturalism spilt over into the classroom?

It has spilt over into the classroom. The whole phenomenon of political correctness, which has invaded British education too, is a product of this. There is a notion that you should not say something that hurts anybody's feelings or any group's feelings. In Britain you have a Race Relations Law, we do not have that here. We believe in the First Amendment of the Constitution, the Bill of Rights, and the First Amendment, which as Justice Oliver Wendell Holmes said, means not only freedom for that with which we agree. There's no virtue in that, but it must mean freedom for the beliefs we hate. It is our belief in the United States that you do not suppress free speech. The best way to deal with speech you hate is for more freedom of speech and not repression. And so the whole doctrine of political correctness is in opposition to the First Amendment of the

Constitution. Political correctness has had some support in the universities, particularly among the radical intellectuals of the 1960s for whom liberalism was always the enemy. The New Left of the 1960s hated liberals much more than they hated conservatives, and similarly today they don't like liberal democracy. They don't like free speech and they want to repress it in the interests of various things. Oddly enough the locus of political correctness in American universities is in the Departments of Literature. Historians are very stalwart in this, they do not go in for political correctness. It is the English departments which seem to be the source of the trouble. However, I think political correctness in the university is a pop fashion that will self-destruct. I'm much more concerned about what is happening in the public schools. As I said, the public schools have been historically the great agency of pulling the country together, and it's the invasion of the public school curricula by multiculturalism in the pernicious sense that is more disturbing than the political correctness nonsense in universities.

If I ask you to identify the most striking changes in American life over the time that you have been in academic and political life, what would you point to?

Oh, the most striking change obviously is in the racial situation. If anyone had told me half a century ago that a Black man would be Chairman of the Joint Chiefs of Staff, and that there'd be Black Justices of the Supreme Court, or there would be a Black Governor of Virginia, the stronghold of the old Confederacy, and that there'd be Black Mayors in Birmingham, Alabama and New Orleans, as well as Atlanta – all southern cities – as well as in New York, Los Angeles, Chicago, Detroit, Philadelphia, and all this while Blacks are still only 12 per cent of the population, I would have been astounded and incredulous. So, while we clearly still have a long distance to go, to destroy the curse of racism, the changes that have been made in my lifetime have been very striking.

There are also other things, the bursting out of the closet of homosexuality is something one cannot ever have anticipated. At least I never anticipated it. And there have been other lifestyle changes. I can remember in 1939 when David L. Selznick, the movie producer, had a great fight with the Hays office before he was permitted to have Clark Gable say in *Gone with the Wind*, 'Frankly, my dear, I don't give a damn.' Damn was a forbidden word, now every movie I see, 'fuck' and 'shit' and so on.

A final question about your own professional career, do you feel satisifed with what you've done?

I do not feel satisfied with what I've done, I feel I've dissipated far too much time and energy in transient and forgotten external causes, and since my chief interest is history and my chief desire is to write history, I feel I have not done justice to myself at all in this regard, and I'm trying to reform.

I am sure there will be many of your readers who will be very surprised by that remark, but anyway thank you very much Professor Schlesinger.

Hugh Sidey

When did you start your career as a Washington correspondent?

I came to Washington in 1957 from New York City where I worked for *Life Magazine* and the first story I covered was President Dwight Eisenhower's second Inaugural, and I've been here ever since. So it's mounting up now, I guess that I have more or less covered the White House for 36 years. *Life Magazine* in those days didn't have a permanent beat but we were there as much as we were elsewhere, so we covered Eisenhower's Suez crisis, the U2 crisis, the civil rights upheavals, the congressional campaigns of 1958 and then the 1960 presidential campaign.

   We covered Eisenhower's illnesses and then the beginning with Kennedy. I switched to *Time Magazine* about that time and began to cover politics and the election of 1960. I got to know those people; as a matter of fact that network of people is still somewhat in place in Washington. I'm talking about those who were associated with Lyndon Johnson, Stuart Symington, Hubert Humphrey; Teddy Kennedy was in that campaign, John Kennedy, Bob Kennedy, Nixon, that whole group. It is remarkable how those young people of that time have gone on. I became the White House correspondent when Kennedy went into the White House and did that for about eight or nine years. I was appointed Bureau Chief of *Time* in DC for another eight or nine years and then I started to do a column for *Life Magazine* called 'The Presidency' and when *Life Magazine* folded I was asked to switch that to *Time*. I have been doing that ever since, basically, and I'm now what you call a Contributing Editor here in Washington, still, more or less, writing about presidents and the events around the White House.

Well, that's a remarkable career. You've spent a considerable amount of time in DC, so what do you think has been the major changes in the politics of the United States during that period?

Well, I would have to say the end of the Cold War of course. But I would have to say in my world of covering presidents and the White House, the biggest change is the media. The sheer size of it now pervades the entire world and the immediacy is remarkable. The satellite, the mini-cam, instantaneous communication has revolutionised politics more than anything and never better illustrated than today with Bill Clinton.

How would you specifically illustrate these changes?

Well, let me go back a little if I can, back to 1957 when I was a young reporter for *Life Magazine*, and we would have a week's news of the White House with Eisenhower. There were about 20 regular White House correspondents in those days and we would go over to Jim Hagerty, who was then Press Secretary, and we would stand around his desk and on many days he would come down and say, 'Sorry boys, no news', and that was the end of it. And we would go off, take a nap, have lunch, never come back. There wasn't the requirement that somehow the President have a performance on the night news, or events in the White House be made into a mini-drama for the evening news. The White House was one section of Government. I can recall during the U2 crisis Hagerty told us very briefly about it and then said for details go to the Pentagon because they knew all about it. And so we went to the Pentagon. We left the White House. Eisenhower went back to the putting green or whatever he did on the south lawn, and we pursued that story elsewhere. Slowly that changed. Kennedy introduced an element of show business in it. Television then began to get bigger. At some point Kennedy realised that the *New York Times, Time Magazine, Life Magazine*, were not the only way to get his word out across the world. And so that began to change.

Lyndon Johnson brought all of the public relations operations into the White House. He decided that all the good announcements would be made from the White House, the bad ones would be made out in the departments, and that tended to centralise it even more. And about this time it began to get personal. The White House became a soap opera. You know it became a drama. This man, his family, his dogs, were all wide open for scrutiny and it slowly built on itself up until this time where we have Bill Clinton. I think the dominant activity now in the White House is dealing with communication to the world, with the media, through talk shows, through his friendships with Hollywood people, through the White House press corps, that's his major activity. I think he spends far more time on talking, persuading, educating, than he does on formulating policy. In fact I would have to say it appears to me that it's quite evident that he's thought a good deal more about communication than about what he is communicating. But anyway, we now have, on a normal day, 150 or 200 correspondents. Marlon Fitzwater, the Press Secretary for George Bush, said that whereas I and my colleagues back in the 1950s had one brief stop during the day, where we'd digest the news, it's now every 15 minutes in the White House. These people with CNN and the TV networks demand a refresher every 15 minutes. So it's a continuous process. Two hundred people, cameras live continuously, the demands of special interviews, special programmes, pressing all the time, and that's day and night at the White House. The White House has been shaped by that, and there's no way to get away from it.

In your view, has that been a good development?

Well, there are moments when it is good, and there are moments when it's bad, but I'm not quite certain. We are sorting it out at this point. I look at it in the short run and there's some grave distortion. I don't know if you know Sam Donaldson, a very good reporter, very aggressive, a little obnoxious, but that's part of the business. Sam was a White House correspondent for about 12 years. He began with Jimmy Carter and spent four years with Carter, and eight years covering Reagan. Sam changed the White House correspondent's role I think more than any other person. Sam brought show business in, and I don't think Sam Donaldson was primarily interested in news, or enlightening people. He was interested in confrontation, in a drama every day, and it became his job to kind of befuddle or confront Ronald Reagan or Jimmy Carter, and then to come in at night with this little give and take that would either show how ill-prepared or inarticulate, or how confused the President was. Then Sam would interject, that became kind of the dominant format for White House coverage, but I think it took some sinister turns. The idea was you had to be terribly negative, you had to embarrass the President, you had to show what a fool he was, you had to show where he was wrong. Some of those press conferences, and a matter of fact they're still that way today, are non-news events. The great press conferences where we used to get out facts, don't really mean that much today, because what you have is 150 to 200 reporters preparing questions that they aren't going to get answered and they know they aren't going to get answered, at least in a frank and open manner. But they're trying to do what Sam Donaldson did, they are trying to flummox the President, and so for a half an hour they ask these questions and then of course the President wants to avoid answering them, but to appear articulate and so he talks and no news generally comes out. So we have this kind of stand off. I think that's evil, I think that's a perversion of what should happen.

Now I think what may save the world ultimately is the satellite, the mini-cam. It's hard to be a tyrant in this world. I mean we have seen that recently. The Sadam Husseins have a difficult time; you can't cover it up any more. Natural calamities are quickly known, torture, disaster of all kinds, instantly known. Like the nuclear plant blow up in the Soviet Union; I think that it is good to bring the sunlight in. And so in the long run I see good, but it's such a powerful thing that there are days when the President of the United States does not control foreign policy. It is controlled by the television networks, or CNN.

Do you think that's put an enormous onus on presidents to be able to deal with the media? Have some presidents been much better than others in your experience?

I think that's the shaping pattern in today's world. There isn't any question, in my mind, that one of the reasons that George Bush lost was his inarticulateness and his inability to talk about his record and what he had done. He was not a bad president by a long shot. His foreign policy I thought, by and large, was excellent. His domestic policy, given that he's a Republican, a conservative and against big government, was quite satisfactory. But when it came down to communicating that and convincing people of his record and the legitimacy thereof, he didn't do it well. Now, Bill Clinton can talk; he is very bright and knowledgeable, he is a man of this age that loves to schmooze and talk and go to think-tanks, seminars, the Harvard Kennedy School, trade missions, talk, talk, talk, words, words, words. A lot of them are not very meaningful, but soothing, some of the words are quite knowledgeable because he does know the material. I think that was a big thing in Clinton's victory, and he was able to do it better than others.

How about some other presidents?

Well, Ike was inarticulate as you know. Some of his sentences were the length of a novel. They didn't have subjects, verbs or objects and if they were present they were not in the right order. Jim Hagerty would have to spend two weeks deciphering these things for us, and as a matter of fact not until the end did Eisenhower allow direct quotation in his press conferences. People have forgotten that it all had to be paraphrased. So you had to make sense out of it and sometimes it was a struggle. Kennedy was articulate, he could handle it. As a matter of fact, just the other day I looked back at those old press conferences of his and they are still the best. Clinton can't hold a candle to him. JFK had true wit, and he had true self-effacing humour. Kennedy could laugh at himself and laugh at issues in a kind of serious fashion. There was a wryness to it. He was very good at it; he knew the subject matter. He was a tough man, a serious man, but with wit, charm and grace and was very well spoken. Without question he ushered in this age of television.

Then we had Lyndon Johnson who was just terrible sometimes. When he was natural he was pretty good but he felt so inferior because he didn't have a Harvard education. He had a chip on his shoulder. So he would try to be as provincial as possible. He would emphasise his accent and talk about your poor 'corn pone' President and all that stuff you know. It just turned people off. He didn't need this and he should have known because of Harry Truman. I didn't cover President Truman, but he never felt inferior. Here's the guy, the only one, not the only one in history, but the only one this century without a college education. He only had a high school education, a former dirt farmer; but confident enough in his own ability that he was never intimidated. His best friend was Dean Acheson, the Yale patrician, but Truman never lorded it over him and didn't try to rub it in. Johnson couldn't do that, so Johnson had a hard time. You know, he looked funny on television, he'd get sore you know. He hated those questions, nasty questions about Vietnam, which was a hard, hard time, and he didn't know how to handle that. It didn't work very well.

Nixon was pretty good. The strength of Nixon was his mind; he wasn't a natural orator. In fact sometimes he got uncoordinated. I remember watching some of his speeches when his hands and his mouth and his words would get out of sync. He'd be talking about some great disaster and he'd be smiling, you know the mouth had gotten there before the head, I can remember that. But there was a power in Nixon's oratory. Here is a serious man who had studied policy and particularly foreign policy. He could talk about it for an hour without notes, and he knew what he was talking about. He had good ideas and I think the sheer power of his mind was his major strength.

Gerry Ford was kind of inarticulate. He didn't expect to be President and wasn't bad really, not as bad as people remember, but still not all that good. Jimmy Carter wasn't all that good either, had an edge to his voice. Jimmy Carter was too self-righteous. He was a preacher, and you know they just love sin, just love to feel bad and that came across in Carter's approach and it didn't do very well. Reagan kind of brought it back to the Kennedy period. He was very powerful and very good, but he just didn't know the details. You know, some days he wasn't quite sure where he was, and he was never over-burdened by fact when he was talking about matters, but when he had a script, and it was one of those subjects that he'd devoted his life to, a strong military machine, fewer taxes, less government, less regulation, old time values, Reagan was as good as you could get. He had that wonderful twinkle and sense of humour and again he had a gravitas. I remember when they allowed him to speak to the Soviet people over television the first time and he gave what I consider was an average speech. But the Washington Post interviewed people on the street and one woman said that she had been told all her life that Ronald Reagan was an evil man, and she said, 'I watched that speech, I looked at his face, I listened to what he said, that is not an evil man that I heard.' He could convince people, he could bring people along.

Bush was good in private sessions but not in that general way. He just didn't have that. Now with Clinton we're back again to some skill, but at this point that the jury's still out on how it's going to work because he may actually talk too much. He may be too serious and too enmeshed in detail, we'll see about that.

One of the things that strikes me about Washington over the last several decades is that the media has become much more intrusive. The personal details of the lives of Eisenhower and Kennedy were never investigated, but the press now appears to be voracious in its appetite for the detail of the lives of politicians in general and the President in particular.

Well, that is directly related to that explosion in media. I mean there are many facets of it; there is just the need for material and then, of course, finding that the most powerful man in the world is an interesting human, with an interesting wife, kids, friends, everything and he also has a profound effect on your life. If this fellow's somewhat deranged it is a matter of public interest and I confess I agree with one of Lyndon Johnson's old speech writers, Richard Goodwin, who suggested that there were moments when Lyndon Johnson was out of touch with reality and that his mental condition was unstable and that Johnson was manic, according to Goodwin, and though it can't be proven, I tend to agree that there were such moments. So it is important how you conduct the office, since the office is so pervasive, so powerful, touches everybody's life. The war in Vietnam was a matter of life and death for kids. Then it's quite natural how that evolution came about and then of course Hollywood got into it and said, 'Hey, this is good soap opera, we got dogs out there and you know we've got wayward children and we've got a wife that's ordering the people around the White House, let's get in there.' In a society like ours, in the end there isn't much that you can keep secret.

So was it different in the late fifties and the early sixties? Were the White House Press Corps much closer to the President?

Yes, I think so, there wasn't the hostility that there is now, there isn't any question of that. It's the 'gotcha' journalism that people talk about. You know, we're looking for the pitfalls and the absence of perfection. Howard Baker the former Senator from Tennessee put it very, very astutely. He said, 'You guys search for the "what is perfect", and that's the enemy of "what is just good".' Because you can't find the perfect, we therefore find flaws and we spend an inordinate amount of time doing that, and you know, that's far more interesting, and unfortunately far more fascinating for viewers and readers than if a fellow passes a Bill. It may be boring but it is worthwhile. Unfortunately, journalism has just taken on that flavour of show business. And it's still there, even more so. And Clinton of course figured that out and exploited it. Now, whether he can legislate and get things done, that's another matter but it's a huge part of our life.

But was it a nicer Washington when jounalists knew things but didn't print them because you felt this was not the business of the public?

Well that's right, I kinda got off track there, the fact of it was that I felt and I think my colleagues back in the time of Eisenhower, Truman and Roosevelt felt that we were all in this together. And while there was an adversarial relationship between the President and press corps, nevertheless we wanted him to succeed. If we saw some aberration or some violation of ethics or the law, yes, we'd report it, but not the normal human vagaries and peccadilloes; that was his business. We didn't pick it up. And that went clear back to Roosevelt who as you know had his girlfriend, Lucy Mercer. My old colleague on the White House beat, Merriman Smith – who won his fame as United Press's fellow that ended the press conference. He was the dean of the press corps, and said, 'Thank you Mr. President', on the radio, and he covered the presidency through World War II – and knew that when Roosevelt went up to Hyde Park, the train stopped at a siding in Newark, and that the girl joined Roosevelt. He never reported it. As a matter of fact, I don't think most of the country were aware Roosevelt was in a wheelchair. They didn't know he was disabled, because it was kind of established that we wouldn't do those things because it didn't matter. It was only towards the end when he got terribly ill, that it began to creep out; people could see it in the pictures.

Same thing in Eisenhower's time, although we got into more candour there when he had that first heart attack, and they tried to cover it up for a little while and then they decided, 'Nuts, this is the new age', and they laid out the details of that sort of thing. But even then, there wasn't much stuff about the private lives of Eisenhower and his wife Mamie. There's been a little bit about Kay Summersbee, who had been his driver in Europe during the war, but it was never proven exactly and we kind of ignored it. And of course anybody that knew Senator John F. Kennedy was aware that he was a great ladies man. I mean the circumstantial evidence that I had when I was covering the Senate in those days was overwhelming. There was no doubt about it, but it didn't intrude; it didn't intrude in the politics and it didn't intrude when he was in the White House. I must confess I was surprised at the extent of it, as his involvement has trickled out with other women and friends of his wife. You know it rather shocked me, but as I look back on it I don't recall that it ever got in the way of him being President. And so we just didn't report it. I knew about it and I told my editors about it. I wrote many memos about what happened down in Palm Beach and that sort of thing, when he'd go down, but they didn't run that either. It was, I think, a matter of feeling that unless it manifested itself in policy or in the operations of the White House, then it was a private matter. Now when it came out, we never had any written testimony from the girls or any eye witnesses or anything like that. In other words there was no documentation, no admissions, no photos; that's another intimidating thing, you don't go public unless there's evidence. The thing changed basically, a few years after Kennedy's death, when Senator Frank Church held the hearings in the Senate on the CIA and their activities in South America and elsewhere. What they came up with in the course of their investigations, were the phone records of Sam Giancanna, the mobster from Chicago. In those records, there were calls from Judith Exner, the prostitute who had relationships with Frank Sinatra and Giancanna, to the White House. Then she admitted it. She wrote a book and that's really when the thing fell in. There were no holds barred and then we've had the news stories of course about Senator Gary Hart and of course Bill Clinton.

It appears that politics and show business have somehow merged. Is that a fair observation?

Oh yes, it's a fair observation, and we used to write about it in Kennedy's time but it's only a fragment of what it is now. This Hollywood connection, country music, blues singers, rock and roll, Elvis Presley, soap operas, prime time, situation comedies, it's all connected. Bill Clinton and his generation grew up on the stuff. They know it all. I suspect it was the dominant element of their culture at that time. Bill Clinton was never known as an outdoors man. He didn't play lacrosse or football or baseball. That generation discovered rock and pop music and the world of movies, video; you know, we shaped them. We, the parents of the people of that age, shaped that generation. I suspect he's just reflecting what he knows. Suddenly at the White House we have Barbara Streisand over and Paul Newman. Just the other day I was in the Hays Adams hotel which is directly across from the White House and I saw this rather overweight rather frumpy woman that I swore was a neighbour of mine. She had kind of a common face, smiling, a nice pleasant woman you know and I started to go up to speak to her. I couldn't remember her name but I swore she was a neighbour and I looked over her shoulder just in time and there was Paul Newman. It was Joanne Woodward, Newman's wife and they had just been over to the White House to see the President. Almost every week now this sort of thing takes place. Only today a couple of song writers had been in the Oval Office, and they played a game with the President, whether he could name what was on the flip side of every Elvis Presley recording, and he apparently did very well. He even sang a couple of them. Thank God we didn't have to listen to it, but there it is. In all seriousness, I'm not sure that's bad.

Now look, I think Ronald Reagan got a lot of the ideas about what was right and wrong and noble and commanding and wonderful and majestic out of movies, out of the movie scripts he read. Those were old-fashioned movie scripts, the good guy and the bad guys. That was a huge part of his education because he was not a reader, and he just wasn't a man who studied things very long. And so you could say even back then, Hollywood was shaping things, but there's no question, there's a lot of money out there and Hollywood people are putting it into politics. They're bright people in their own way; they have a lot of ideas how the world should run, mostly liberal, and they're using their influence now. They are focused and they are a dominant part of American culture.

Can I just change the subject slightly? It seems to me that politics itself has become a much bigger deal than it was 35 years ago.

Well again I have to say that's the media. The cost for one thing is because of television. Having to buy time. And once again it's 24 hours a day, 365 days a year on a constant four-year cycle. In other words these campaigns don't stop, as Clinton has demonstrated. It goes on all the time now. A man who wants to be in public life must constantly be on the move and he must be on some screen or in some paper. It's a huge, huge business. I don't believe that anybody's calculated how many billions of dollars are diverted every year into running campaigns. It is a big massive industry in this town. Tens of thousands of people earn their living polling, advising candidates, a very lucrative business. And the media feeds off it, again we cover it. We create the drama in our own way and then we write about it and report it and so we're kind of all in this together, it pervades this city and the government.

When you came to Washington in the late fifties, did you believe that the American political system worked?

Pretty well, I have to say, pretty well. As a matter of fact let me quickly add that I'm not sure it's as bad as we sometimes write it is today. You sit in this city, you read the *Washington Post* and a few other things and you think it's absolutely unworkable. But I go back to Winston Churchill. He said you look at this system, it's the worst possible system except for all those others we have tried. You know what he meant. If you go to New York City and you consider how many people there are and how the system works, you say this is no way to run a city, it won't work. It can't feed all the people, get the waste out, give them all jobs, and yet somehow, at the end of the day, it's gotten through. And so I think the Government still works probably better than a lot of people think, but I think it's more difficult now. I think when I came, there was a greater sense of national purpose. There was more tolerance of each other, less partisanship, there was a shared national interest and I have to say that probably part of that was due to the Cold War and the confrontation with the Soviet Union. We were scared. It kept us focused on the idea that this was a great system, and we'd have to make sacrifices for it and we had to pay taxes to buy missiles and warheads and sometimes we had to go to war to protect our rights. All of these were necessary and that there had to be leadership to achieve it. Honestly, that probably more than any other any single element, the end of the Cold War, probably took the focus out of our national life. I think there are other things happening, but that's the huge one. I can see the development of an underclass in the cities, the problems with civil rights, the assertion of minorities for more rights, the worn-out infrastructure around the country and demands for more public input, these things also contributed to the ending of a common national interest. But I would say the fact that we don't have a devil and we don't have an evil empire any longer, probably more than anything has diffused politics and has confused it.

A final question; this must have been a very sleepy town when you first came here, a small town if not a sleepy town. It no longer feels like that.

Well, I think that changed, but if I want to be really frank about it, then I have to get that from books. I think that changed at the start of World War II, when you had the huge influx of all the big bureaus and the weapons procurement and the growth in the size of the navy and army. I think it was an exciting town then. It didn't have the structure

103

it does now, so you had a lot of little strange places tucked away in temporary barracks and that sort of thing. I think perhaps right after the war there was some kind of sign and people did go home a bit, but I don't think it ever really got back to that day. It's changed in my time, and I can remember almost when it changed. The night Sputnik went up I happened to be covering that night and we were up all night and the town had a kind of an arrogance and self-confidence you know after the war. We had all the money and we had all the nuclear weapons. We had the power. I mean we stood astride the world and people were beholden all over. October 1957 when Sputnik went up, that changed suddenly. The whole attitude that somebody could challenge us. I remember there was a change then. It hadn't really been a sleepy town, but I guess that suddenly we were a bit frightened from then on, up until now. We ran a little scared. Just about the time we'd get a new weapons system and we'd discover the Soviets would have one too, and then we began to run out of money a little. We just couldn't quite find as much wealth as we'd had. It was a different city then, no question. It was simpler. You hadn't developed the huge media complex. We had not developed the immense special interests. Clinton said there were 80,000 people representing special interests in Washington. I think that's crazy, but I've heard 35,000. But maybe he's right, and the special interests have created a huge apparatus here of lobbying, influence pedalling. Lawyers have flocked in. You know we're a litigious society, we sue and so the complexity of it, without question, has changed the nature of this city. It's not as much fun let me tell you.

But you still enjoy it?

Well I still do, but I must say some of these issues absolutely perplex me. I mean trying to work your way through Bosnia for instance, with all of that difficulty. Lord knows what's going to come out when they produce a health-care plan, but I imagine it's going to be one of the most complex operations that this city has ever seen and we've already seen Clinton's proposals for a stimulus package, tax reform and they are terribly complex involving all of these special interests and regions of the country. It is very difficult to govern today, there is no question about it. And that creates more work, more worry, more tension, irritation, so it's a good deal more sombre and I would say a more inefficient, doubting and wondering city than it used to be when I arrived.

Hugh Sidey, thank you very much.

Gloria Steinem

Can I start this conversation by asking you about the role and position of American women as we come to the turn of the century? What do you think have been the major developments over the last several decades?

We've had two major movements in this country since the Europeans arrived. One was, of course, the suffragette and abolitionist movement. I think it's important to remember how recently that was, only 75 years ago, that women were still chattled, were still owned like tables and chairs, and to remember that it took almost 150 years to gain for women of all races a legal identity as citizens and human beings. So having gained in the first wave a legal identity, I think now in this current wave we're striving for a legal equality. And I would say we're maybe 25 years into what, by precedent, will be a century of change. In this last 25 years, we have done a pretty good job of consciousness raising; that is I think there's almost nobody left in the country who doesn't feel differently about what women and men can do and what their children can do, and who doesn't have a general idea that women can do what men can do. However, the difference between consciousness and reality is one that is going to provide us with a lot to do for the next 75 years. We have the idea of equal pay and majority support for it, the idea of equal parenthood – which is a real revolution – the idea of women in high political office, of reproductive freedom as an additional basic human right, all of these are now majority issues. But the power structure, the real way that money is distributed, work is distributed, children are raised, have yet to change. And we have a new consciousness-raising stage to go through which is not just 'women can do what men can do' but 'men can do what women can do', very crucial.

I will return to several of the points that you just mentioned. Can I just ask you whether there are any tangible differences in the experience of being female in the United States in the 1990s as opposed to the 1950s? Are there things that one could point to which are materially different?

I am here to tell you that there is a big difference because, as a fifties person, I was formed in that era and I had absolutely no notion, nor was given any notion by society, or by my textbooks, that I could do other than marry the person I wanted to become, or that biology was not destiny. Or that women had communal interests across boundaries of class and race by virtue of living in a patriarchy. No, that occurred nowhere in the fifties, absolutely nowhere. Now at least we have turned depression to anger, which is a big step forward. We have begun to imagine the world as if women mattered, and you have to imagine something before it can really exist. We have acquired a lot of tools and made a lot of steps forward in a concrete way towards that world.

So what happened to you personally?

Well, alarmingly late. I wish it had happened earlier, but I think, like many women, I went through life identifying with every other group of people who were having a hard time. So I went to live in India for two years right after I got out of college, which had an enormous impact on me. And I, emotionally and intellectually, identified with the Third World, without understanding that women are a Third World wherever we are, low on technology, low on money, on capital, and labour intensive. I identified, when I came home, with the civil rights movement, with the anti-war movement, with the migrant worker movement, but I didn't understand that there was a reason. It was viewed as mysterious by other people that a White, middle-class person would be identifying with these movements, and I didn't understand it either. It wasn't until the feminist light bulb began to come on over all of our heads in the late sixties and early seventies that I understood that women were a seriously disadvantaged and oppressed group too; that there was a reason why we empathised emotionally with other groups similarly situated.

Do you remember what actually made that light shine?

Well I remember one experience in particular but I think I had been gradually beginning to get it a little bit. The pivotal experience for me was as a reporter here for *New York Magazine*. I went to cover a hearing [meeting] that was held in protest of an official abortion hearing in our New York State Legislature. This was before we had a Supreme Court ruling on abortion. So New York State was considering the liberalisation of its abortion laws, and they had invited to testify fourteen men and one woman, one nun. So a group of early feminists said, 'Hey, wait a minute, let's hear from women who have actually had this experience of having to go out into a criminal underground and seek an illegal abortion.' And they held a 'speak out'; a hearing in a church basement downtown. So I went as a reporter to cover this and for the first time in my life I heard women stand up in public and tell the truth, about a socially unacceptable, unconventional act as part of their lives. It was incredibly moving. Just as in the civil rights movement people stood up in Black churches in the South and testified about what had happened to them, it brought tears to hear individuals speak the truth and was something I'll never forget. I also had had an abortion some years before that, actually in London, where the laws were not great then, but better than here. If you had the permission of two physicians you could have an abortion, and I had never told anyone, no one. After I wrote this piece, (which of course I wrote in a very respectable reportorial way, never saying 'I'), it all began to unravel for me. I started to think, 'Wait a minute, you know, if one in three American women statistically has had to seek an abortion at some time in her life, why is it illegal? Why are we controlled as the means of reproduction so to speak? Why is this decision not our own decision?' And from that it is like having a ball of yarn – you pick the end of the skein and suddenly everything starts to unravel. I just began to see. Of course in this country we had before our eyes the example of another caste system. There are many parallels, you know, between sexual caste and racial caste. So we began to see it.

And how did that affect your life? Obviously it had a profound impact. Did it change the course of your career?

Everything. It changed everything, everything. Up to that time, if somebody said to me 'you write like a man', which was a very great compliment, I would say 'thank you'. I couldn't get an apartment

109

because the landlord would think that if I could pay for it I was a hooker and if I wasn't a hooker I couldn't pay for it. I thought somehow that was my fault. If I was having to placate sexually an editor and keep his ago intact but still get an assignment, I thought that was my job. It never occurred to me that maybe I shouldn't have to do that. I probably blamed my mother. I thought that my mother was an exception in some way because she had actually been destroyed and had her spirit broken by growing up in this. She had everything she cared about taken away from her. And, you know, it just suddenly makes sense of your life. People say in this country you only get radicalised on your own concerns. Well, I think that is true. You start to see the politics of your own life, and thus expand as it should be expanded, the definition of politics. It is usually defined in a way to keep us out of it, it is what goes on in the legislature. But actually, politics is any power relationship in our daily lives, any time one group of people is habitually dominant over another, not because of more experience or intelligence or whatever, but simply because of how they got born, whether that's class or race or gender, that's politics. So you start to see it, you know, you go into a department store and you see, wait a minute, why are men selling kitchen ranges, and women are selling men's underwear? This is not expertise. This is commission. This is how much money you get, you just see it wherever you go.

Were there any particular writers or philosophers who were writing about feminism who had an impact on you?

Oh yes, very much so. I read Shulamith Firestone *The Dialectic of Sex* which was brilliant and which just totally blew my mind. Kate Millett too. Simone de Beauvoir was in a different place at that time, in a way, so somehow what she was saying didn't apply so directly to my life. Anne Koedt who wrote an essay called, 'The Myth of the Vaginal Orgasm' suddenly made me think about Freud and the sort of psychic clitoroectomy performed on every woman within his philosophy. It was, it is still, an exciting period but you never forget the first light coming on.

Do you think the role of women in the United States has been particularly problematic or do you think this is true of most Western societies?

I think that patriarchy is a system of maybe five and eight thousand years vintage which is not universal but which seems universal. The exceptions tend to be non-industrial cultures, or very particular examples. The male structure, whether it is religion or a state or a tribe, needs to control women's bodies as the most basic means of production, the means of reproduction. It's been made to seem universal, whether or not it was.

It appears to those living on the other side of the Atlantic, that feminism, which certainly is varied, emerged in the seventies and eighties and seemed very much to be driven by American women. Do you agree?

No, I don't think it's fair actually. I think it's mainly that the media is centred here. Although I would be quite proud to think of feminism as an American export, it would be the only healthy thing we ever exported that I'm aware of! But, in fact, there is a very strong indigenous feminist movement within every culture. It's dangerous for it to be seen as an American export because the whole idea of feminism is self-determination. So if it is perceived as following a colonial pattern, it's a big mistake, a really big mistake.

I didn't quite mean that. I just meant that there were so many American women who were prominent. I just wondered whether it said something about American society that American women were particularly prominent.

Well, I do think that it was very important that we had the example of the civil rights movement before us. This was true, of course, of the suffragette wave too, because we had the example of the abolitionist movement; universal suffrage was something that clearly banded together women of all races and Black men, so that the racial example was very important. I suppose that there are certain things about American society that make this kind of speaking out more possible or probable. We're regarded, probably rightly, as blindly optimistic. We have a least the myth of being able to become who we want to be, regardless of where we're born. We have a class system but it's not quite as air tight as it may be in other places. Then women were more likely to say 'why not?' We have faith in change. This whole nation has been devoted to change, so I'm sure that is part of it too. And then there is the phenomenon of the media of this country with its lust for the new. That means though you get penalised later because you become old news, in the beginning you can at least get an audience for what you're saying.

I take your point that there have been remarkable changes since the fifties, but there's a long way to go.

Oh yes, yes. As a kind of rough gauge, we in this wave, probably by all historical precedent, have at least 75 years to go. We may well have other waves before we achieve societies in which people are regarded as unique individuals and their race or their sex or their class are not somehow used to dictate their futures.

You've been remarkably successful in your professional life. Do you still feel that there are very real constraints on you because you're a woman?

Oh yes absolutely. I realise one story is worth a thousand generalities so I'm trying to think of an example. For instance, I went to campaign in Texas against a woman named Kay Bailey Hutchinson who is the US Senator from Texas. In fact, she won as a Republican, and I was campaigning against her on the issues she is against. For 20 years she has been against reproductive rights, she's against parental leave, against Head Start programmes. There was a man who was, in fact, more of a feminist than she running against her. I got criticised, not just by the right wing, but *USA Today* and some others for campaigning against a woman. And I was very upset by this for a while. And then I thought, 'Well, but if I had been for her, they would have been just as angry because they would have said you're only for her because she's a woman.' So it's that moment when you realise that nothing you do can be right; when you realise that you are part of a group that is supposed to be kept in a subordinate position, and that happens to me just as much as everybody else. Sometimes more so, because I become a symbol of it so people come up to me in the street and say things that they might perhaps otherwise keep to themselves.

So how should things develop? Are these matters of public policy, or are these matters of private consciousness?

Both. You know the motto of the women's movement has been that personal is political. I would also add that political is personal, so it isn't one or the other. Our inner psyches, if we've been born into a subordinate group, are quite crippled sometimes. It's as if inside us was a garden growing in the shadow for so long that even after you took the barrier away it still grew in the same pattern. So if you get a group of women together, they may very well punish the strong member of the group, just as a group of men may punish the the weak member. That is the way gender roles are policed. And so to get up and out of that we constantly need each other's support; we need to examine what we are doing. Private consciousness or small group or communal consciousness is the beginning of everything. Public policy is the fruit of that effort. If it isn't, it won't work because people can't be given power, they can only take it. Just as many wonderful rights can exist on paper and be meaningless, policy has to come as a result of the individuals strengthening themselves.

It seems to be again, as an observer from across the Atlantic, that a lot of the ideas you are writing about fell on very fertile ground in the late sixties and throughout the seventies, but certainly in recent years, society hasn't been so receptive. Many people feel that feminism has gone too far. Is that a sense you have as well?

I think that when a movement begins, you can march forward without a backlash, but when you come to be a little bit successful, then you have a backlash. That is what happened to us in the eighties. In a sense it's a tribute to success, otherwise we wouldn't have had a backlash. But unfortunately because most people in this country don't vote, our backlash elected Reagan then Bush, the two most anti-equality Presidents this country has ever seen. And it's because we ourselves look at the newspapers and the television that we think these ridiculous guys represent the country, which by no public opinion poll they do, on issues of equality. We ourselves get discouraged. You know it's a sort of trick to undermine what is actually a majority changed consciousness. So the backlash, which was partly an economic one on the part of many companies who were benefiting from the fact that women were making 65, 70 cents on the dollar, while they were pocketing the rest. And part of it was religious too. There is a very fine line there because I think patriarchal religion is just a way of making a ruling class sacred. We have our ayatollahs here, you know. We have the head of the Mormon church and we have the Catholic Bishops. I always think of them as the people our European ancestors came here to escape! They are completely forthright authoritarian folks, and they got themselves together and they have 9000 fundamentalist Baptist churches, not to mention all the other denominations. We don't have 9000 anything, they are much more rooted. We were much newer. And so the eighties became a time of trying of running very hard to stay in place against this right-wing backlash.

But whatever their power it seems to me that some changes are just inexorable. The percentage of young women going to university and going on to graduate school, and joining the professions is a flood which simply cannot be controlled by those who are trying to control it.

I hope you are right but I think nothing is inexorable. I think everything depends on what you and I do every day, because we've seen other advances turned backward. For instance, during World War II, because women were needed as labourers in the factories and in all kinds of jobs men work traditionally at, women got quite uppity and so on. But we were still put in our place right after the war because the men came home. And suddenly there was this whole ethos of togetherness and suburban whatever, you know. And it was quite successful in forcing women out of the labour force. Although women are much better educated than we used to be, it's also true that our unemployed and under-employed are becoming better educated every year. Females still need to have lots of degrees, but guys who are office boys sometimes become president of the company. So you know the insistence on paper degrees is something that differentially effects insurgent groups, and women too.

But nevertheless there have been remarkable changes, and do you take any sense of pride in that?

Oh yes, yes, yes, yes. If I were not an optimist, I probably wouldn't be a movement person in the first place. It gives me such joy and satisfaction to see people blossoming and changing and being almost reborn. Or born for the first time, by being able to use their talents, and to stand up for themselves and to be the unique people that they truly are. I go to some little mining town in East Texas and there is a feminist group meeting in the roadhouse on Route 99. One woman is a sheriff, somebody else is the wife of the local oil man, somebody else is the short-order cook. And what are they doing? Teaching women who are on welfare how to work in an all-male occupation and how to get off welfare. There is a really exciting cross-class, cross-race kind of reaching out and supporting each other and it's a constant joy. If it weren't for that, I would have perished long ago.

Do you take pride in the fact that you yourself might have had some impact?

Oh yes, yes, absolutely. I take equal pride in two things. One is that I've contributed in a unique way, and the other is that if I were to get hit by a truck tomorrow it would go right on. Because that is equally important.

How do you feel about your career, about what you've done? Do you look back on it and think you've done as much as you could have done, as much as you have wanted to do?

No. I think I could have done it all faster. I often kept on doing what I already knew how to do, instead of moving forward. And I am lately finding, as I approach 60 next year, that this is true even of my defiance, a part of myself which I cherish. Defiance is a very healthy emotion and you can get a long way on defiance. But mine always takes the form of saying, 'I'm just gonna go right on doing everything I was doing before. I don't care if they tell me that you're not supposed to do it at your age.' But then I began to realise that's not progress. So the task and the joy is to stay constantly open to the idea that nothing will be the same tomorrow as it was yesterday. You need to have one hand open to receive all that is coming in, in terms of change, and the other hand closed to hang on to the strength that you need. But they can't both be closed.

Gloria Steinem, thank you very much.

Henry Waxman

Can I begin this conversation by asking you what it was like to grow up in the Los Angeles of the 1940s?

I grew up in East Los Angeles which was a Jewish neighbourhood and was turning very quickly into a Mexican American area. We then moved to South Central Los Angeles where we lived above my father's grocery store. That neighbourhood was also a diverse one because it was not in any way a Jewish neighbourhood. It was mixed racially and ethnically and I stayed there until I graduated from high school.

Did you enjoy the ethnic mix?

I did, although this was a time when the disgraceful chapter in American history of segregation was coming to an end. We didn't have official segregation in the west coast of the United States. But in 1954, when I was in high school, the US Supreme Court came down with the landmark decision that said that separate, even if equal, was not acceptable and it was an enormous boost to everyone. We all felt that we needed to remove the barriers for people to succeed in American society and the barrier of race or religion or any other kind of discrimination was so unfair. So we all felt a sense of optimism, that these antiquated ways would go away and we would have a better society in the United States, when individuals would be permitted to succeed to their fullest extent possible without being hindered or held back because of discrimination.

Do you think that Jewish Americans have a particularly strong feeling of kinship for Blacks and civil rights generally?

Jewish Americans have experienced for hundreds, if not thousands, of years a discrimination in one part of the world or another and I think we felt even more keenly that the discrimination against anybody is wrong if it's based on some extraneous factor, like race or ethnic origin or sex, and now many are even talking openly about sexual preference being an unfair discrimination as well. I think from a Jewish point of view it's not only based on our experience of having been the victims of discrimination but in the sense that to be a just society, to try to make this a better world, we need to give people the opportunity to succeed and to move forward and to be productive.

Is your Jewish heritage very important to you?

It is very important to me. I have a real sense of heritage and tradition that puts me pretty clearly in a whole stream of history, but also gives me a sense of values that I think are important in my day-to-day life. These values help with not only my own personal decisions but for a public policy position I have to make decisions as a member of the United States Congress.

So when did you decide that you wanted a career in political and public life?

I was always interested in politics and government since the time I was quite young. My family took an active interest in what was going on in the community in which we lived. My parents had lived through the Great Depression in the United States during the 1930s and had a very strong reverence for President Franklin Roosevelt. They felt that the New Deal under Roosevelt was a way the government could help people succeed, and protect the working people from the hard edges of a capitalist system which, if left unchecked, would allow employers to take advantage of their employees. Also consumers could be taken advantage of by those who would try to get financial benefits without always delivering what they claimed to deliver. Politics and government was a way to bring about greater justice for everybody and a better society in which everyone could enjoy the benefits of a prosperous nation, a society that treated people more fairly.

So your political consciousness was developed fairly early on?

I would say that my political consciousness was pretty well determined from early experiences, and I really haven't had too much since then to sway me from the basic philosophical point of view in which I approach matters. I strongly believe – and it's one reason I am in politics today – that government can play, and must play, a very appropriate and important role, otherwise large numbers of people will suffer as a result. I guess over the years I've changed some of my views on some specifics, but generally my philosophical way of looking at things is very much that we shouldn't turn to a *laissez-faire* society. I strongly support a capitalist economic system, but I think some of the rough edges of that capitalist system have to be rounded off with a government that will make competition really continue to work, and not allow monopolies to result, and will also empower consumers to be able to be treated fairly in the market-place.

Were you active in politics at university?

I was active in the Democratic party when I was a student at the university. I wasn't active in student government but more involved in political battles in the state of California.

So what was your first position in elective office and how did that come about?

I was elected to the state legislature in California at the age of 28. I ran in a campaign when no one thought I could possibly win because I challenged an incumbent in my own Democratic party. We have a primary system where we don't just turn to the party leaders but to those who are registered and active and willing to vote. This particular incumbent had lost touch with his district. I ran on a very meagre budget with a very strong grass-roots campaign; I personally walked door to door and met many voters, and ended up winning that election with the largest margin that an incumbent in his own party had ever been defeated by for the legislature in California.

Did you enjoy your time in the legislature?

I enjoy the legislation and the legislative responsibility more than I do the political campaigning part of my job. Happily I haven't really had a tough election since 1960 when I was first elected to the California state legislature. I decided that while I believed government had an important role to play, there was uncertainty as to what role it ought to play in some areas. But when it came to health, I thought it was indisputable that government was involved, to make sure that people had access to health care. I signed on to the legislative health committee in California and then when I came to Congress I sought assignment to the committee that had the jurisdiction over health issues and, soon thereafter became Chairman here in the Congress of the United States.

Why did you decide to run for the Congress? Why did you decide you wanted to leave the legislature of California?

In California, as in every state, there is a census every 10 years. As a result, there is a readjustment of the legislature to reflect equal populations in those districts. There was a congressional district which overlapped a lot of the area I had already represented in the state legislature, without a strong candidate or an incumbent and so it was neat and logical step for me to make my move at that time. When I ran for Congress in 1974, after this re-districting, I really didn't have much of an opposition to run for that office. I think people assumed that I was a popular enough state legislator and that none of the other formidable candidates would really have a chance to win.

So you now find yourself in Congress in early 1975; was it an enormous change in your life?

Well in 1975 you have to recognise what was going on historically. It was a time when the Watergate scandal in the United States had brought down President Nixon. He was forced to resign in August of 1974. The election in November of that year brought a sweep of Democrats into the Congress. We had a heavy Democratic margin, many of the Democrats that were elected were reform-minded, as was I, and wanted to change a lot of what was going on in government at that time. We wanted to redress the imbalance between the executive and the legislative branch of government. At that time many people talked about an imperial presidency, not only because of Richard Nixon, but also because of Lyndon Johnson's behaviour. Both President Johnson and President Nixon pursued the war in Vietnam without ever getting a declaration of war from the Congress, and they pursued the war even though popular sentiment had turned strongly against it. I ran in the election as an anti-war candidate. I thought it was a mistake for the United States to pursue the war in Vietnam and wanted us to stop it and to take away some of the power that had gone to the President which permitted him to act so unilaterally in so many important areas. The second area of reform dealt with the seniority system in the Congress. The seniority system which is still in effect today in a modified form, allows the person who has served the longest on a committee in the House or the Senate, to become chairman if he or she is in the majority party, without regard to that individual's ability. As a consequence at that time there were many southern Democrats who had been in office for decades, who became chairman of committees because the safest congressional districts in the country were in the south. These chairmen were quite autocratic, in many cases. They refused for a generation to allow civil rights laws to move to a vote of the full house and Senate, because these southern Democrats were against civil rights. They blocked other social legislation even though there was a majority in the Congress to support some of these programmes. Everyone had been frustrated including President Kennedy and President Johnson. So we took on the seniority system after the 1974 election and made clear to committee chairmen that they had to answer to their own party, in our case the Democratic party, and get a majority vote of the Democrats in order to stay on as a committee chairman. We felt that if they didn't have the support of the majority we would then choose someone else to take their place. Of course that had a monumental affect on the way the seniority system operated because chairmen could not continue to be autocratic without worrying about the fact that at some point a majority of his own party may decide that he or she was not acting in the interests of the party to someone else.

You arrived in the Congress in the early seventies and you've been here some 20 years; have you always been very focused?

I've always felt there is an important role for government to play and a lot of what I have done over the years has been in the health or the environmental area. The role for government is so obvious. I championed the research done through the National Institutes of Health, because I know that unless government funds research activities we really will not have those activities funded, and the hopes for the future to prevent, control and even cure dreaded diseases would be impaired. I've championed the national health insurance which we hope will be accomplished now that President Clinton has made it front and centre of his administration's objectives, but I've always felt that every American ought to have access to health care. Whenever I've travelled around the world and gone to other countries that have national health insurance systems, whether they are conservative or liberal, people have turned to me and said, 'How can you have a health-care system where your country pays more for health care than any in the world and yet you leave so many millions of people without any access to care?' I think it's a crazy system that we have in the United States and it's unjust. So I've long championed trying to get people more access to care. I authored changes in the law that would expand the two existing programmes that are in place. One is called Medicare which covers the elderly and disabled, and the other is the Medicard programme which covers the very poor. During the 1980s we were able to expand both programmes, particularly Medicard, by including more low income women and children to get prenatal and infant care services. Now all children up to the age of 18 get the medical services that are needed. These reforms have met the obvious need for people to get care until we put in place a system that is going to put all Americans in this system together and not just those who could afford to buy themselves health care.

Aids is an issue of some considerable concern to you; could you tell us a little bit about your experience and record in this area?

In 1981, when the first cases emerged in Los Angeles and San Fransisco in the gay community, I got involved to try to find out what was going on. I represented the Los Angeles area where there is a large gay community, and also as the person in charge of health issues, it seemed to me something was going on. None of us could have predicted the scale and growth of the disease. It was and is very very troubling. I would have hoped when we found out about Aids, that the government response would have been more activist. We tried to get the Reagan administration to put more money into research and to try to fight the disease on a number of different levels. We found tremendous resistance from the administration, because of the fact that they were so indifferent to it, due to the kinds of people who were getting Aids, gay men, for the most part, and drug abusers. The Reagan administration responded to the right wingers on social issues and they didn't want to deal with this disease the way they would have if it was a socially accepted population group that was being infected and dying so rapidly. It seems to me incredible that we had to fight President Reagan for so many years before he would even mention the word Aids. The administration's response was tepid.

In the Congress we had to fight for additional funds for Aids research. We added more and more to the budget that was presented to us, because they didn't want to deal with this epidemic. They didn't want to deal with it because they didn't want to spend money on it, on any domestic issue and they didn't want to spend money particularly for a population that they didn't approve of. I think that we have suffered enormously because of the unwillingness of the people in leadership to take on the fight. Even today we're struggling with getting enough funds to do the testing and counselling of people who may be infected. We've tried to do more in the area of research and we put a great deal of money into it. We still have not been successful, which makes one think that we've got to do more in the area of prevention, but we've been hounded by those in this country who don't want to honestly tell Americans that Aids is sexually transmitted for fear that if they had this information, they might engage in sexual practices that they might not otherwise have thought of. It's an incredibly naïve point of view, but that has hurt us throughout this Aids epidemic. Our anti-Aids prevention efforts have been tepid. It is only recently that we have started talking honestly about condoms. To be effective, I think Aids awareness has to be focused on those groups that are most likely to be infected, and yet we still have a fear in this country of saying to homosexual men, 'use condoms', or to drug users, 'don't share needles'.

What makes an effective member of Congress?

I've always felt that to be effective, it helps to try to stay focused on certain objectives that you try to accomplish. Many of my colleagues get involved in so many different issues, that I sometimes think they have no effect on any. I have a broad interest on a whole range of issues. But because I have tried to spend my time on health and environmental issues, I think I've been more successful in accomplishing legislative objectives and bringing about social changes.

You've been here some 20 years a Congressman; what have been the greatest changes that you've observed in Washington?

We've gone through a lot in the past 20 years. We've ended the Vietnam war. We had the Watergate crisis and its aftermath which has shaken, even to this day, the confidence that people have that government is there to represent them and to serve their interests. Before the Nixon presidency, most people thought government acted for them and they gave the president and members of Congress a great deal of the benefit of the doubt that they were going to try to do what was right for the country. But I think we've been facing a tremendous amount of cynicism in the last 20 years. It's grown ever since President Nixon. In addition, there is a sense that government can't answer problems and that people in public office are not trying to solve problems. I think the public attitude towards people in public office is not one of high esteem. The people feel that politicians don't really represent their constituents or public interests but rather special interests, which are always fighting for advantage in the legislative battles.

The issues front and centre have changed, because during the 1980s, after President Reagan came into power, there was a dramatic move to the right. The budget deficit grew extraordinarily after President Reagan decided he would rely on a supply-side economic theory, which gave tax breaks to the very, very wealthy, and spent even more money than we had ever before on defence and that this would move the economy forward. The Reagan administration claimed that we would close the deficit because we'd be so prosperous. The wealth of the people on top grew quite a bit, but it didn't lead to a more productive distribution of that wealth. It concentrated the wealth in fewer and fewer hands. In the 12 years of the Reagan and Bush administrations, we've seen a growing disparity between the haves and have nots. I think we have moved away from a lot of that idealism that the American people genuinely felt about what we could achieve as a country. The optimism that we could get results and that we could get everybody moving forward, lifting up those on the bottom without hurting those on the top. Instead we now have a situation in the United States which is really remarkable because those who can afford services are buying them, leaving those who have to rely on the public sector to go without. For example, we have always had a strong sense of pride in the United States over our public education system. Everyone went to public schools when I grew up. Perhaps the children of extremely wealthy people went to private schools, but I didn't know too many of those folks anyway. But nearly everyone went to excellent public schools. It became a way for social advancement for everyone. Today we have people hiring their own police force which was quite unheard of. Those who can afford to hire their own police will not want to spend money for the rest of the people to be protected. Then it seems to me we're eroding one of the basic reasons we have a government and an organised society. I talked to a friend of mine recently who had been a judge in California for a number of years and worked for the Los Angeles court. He told me that he now was going to become a judge for private parties who would hire him to adjudicate their disputes, because these private parties didn't want to wait to go to court. Well, if we allow people to hire their own judges, you wonder what that means for those who are going to rely on the judicial system. These trends in the last 20 years have really disturbed me. Of course it feeds the cynicism about government, because government services deteriorate when they're not available to everyone, or when everyone doesn't feel [they have] a stake in what the government does. It lends credibility to those who say, well I guess government can't do anything right because we have poor people's programmes and poor people are still poor.

You are in the middle of a very successful political career; what are your ambitions?

I'm enjoying the challenge of being a Congressman, because to me it's an opportunity to try to make advances, to try to deal with problems that can be corrected. I do know that I have made a difference in the lives of millions of people that I'll never meet. When low income women and their children get health-care services, which may well save their lives, I can have a sense of satisfaction.

I've worked on environmental issues, like the Clean Air Act, which has been a successful law and which has been successful in reducing the pollution in the air. It means the US is a healthier place for people to live.

I authored a bill to give greater incentives to the development of what are called orphan drugs and these are drugs for people with rare diseases. Without that legislation, a couple of hundred new products wouldn't be available for people who otherwise would have had to wait for the pharmaceutical industry to get around to their problems when they didn't offer a real profit, since there were so few people involved. These diseases became orphans which meant that no company wanted to spend the time to develop research and manufacture products that could help these people fight back against their diseases.

The debates over abortion, I think have been really quite poisonous. There's a strong debate over whether people ought to be permitted to have an abortion. I think it's a decision that shouldn't be made by government. While I strongly support government making a difference in people's lives, I think there's a limit as to how intrusive government should be in people's private decisions. Abortion is a medical procedure. It is a legal one and is constitutionally protected in this country. Yet we've had many people who've tried to restrict it. But they've carried the debate on abortion policy in to areas where it's been quite destructive and inappropriate. For example, President Bush put a ban on research involving the transplantation of foetal tissue, which holds out hope for people with Parkinson's disease, Alzheimer's disease and diabetes. Because the most extremist groups that were against abortion didn't want the foetal tissue of a dead foetus to be used for research, he in effect told these people that they would have to continue suffering from their diseases, because they were going to take all this foetal tissue and burn it or buy it, and not use it to save people's lives. The second example of this poisonous abortion issue was in the clinics to encourage contraception. President Reagan and President Bush wanted to put restrictions in place that would keep doctors even from telling young women in these clinics that abortion was an option if they turned out to be pregnant. To not disclose all the legal options available to people seems to me to be malpractice and a violation of free speech. It is also condescending and insulting. But that ban which was put in place, called the 'gag rule', was something we tried to overturn, and finally succeeded in doing when President Clinton came into office.

Is there something specific that you would like to achieve in the next few years?

I would find it a tremendous satisfaction if I could be an important part of developing a national insurance system. I've worked piecemeal on the problem and expanded health-care services for many needy people, but if we can then put into place a system that was fair and just provided life-saving and health-enhancing services for everyone, I would feel that would be an enormous accomplishment. I am very excited at the fact that, after many, many years, I have a President of my own party who wants to achieve some of these very same goals. When I served in the California legislature Republican Ronald Reagan was governor, and when I was elected back to the House of Representative in Washington, apart for a few years when Jim Carter was President, Ronald Reagan was back here again. George Bush was President for a short time and Gerald Ford succeeded President Nixon. But now the Clinton administration is here and I have hopes that we get on and address so many of these important issues that have been neglected for so long. Problems can get worse and after while people start to think perhaps nothing can be done about it. Perhaps we have to accept the fact that there are large numbers of people that are homeless in our society, even though this is the most prosperous country in the history of the world. Maybe we just have to accept the fact that there's going to be an underclass that's permanent and may be growing which has lost hope of any chance for advancement. This has led, I think, not only to desperation of those who are living under those circumstances, but to a growing rate of crime, which is a major concern to everyone. But these problems can be addressed. There are no easy solutions, but to give up and to not even try seems to me to condemn us to the continued pattern of so many people becoming more and more desperate at being left out of society. We'll become like so many Third World countries where the elite, the well to do, have wonderful lives. They are always surrounded by security forces to protect them from the masses, who have to be kept repressed, in order to keep their desires in check. America has always been a great country because we've had a strong middle class. I've gone to other countries like Argentina, for example, where they too went through the turmoils of the Great Depression at the same time as us, but they moved in a different direction; they turned to Peron, the dictator, which meant that Argentina, which had natural resources equal to most countries, and at that time before the depression, one of the highest standards of living of any nation, sunk to Third World status within a few decades. I look at the United States and realise that we avoided that not because of genetic brilliance on the part of the people that moved to the United States, as opposed to South America, but because we had wise leadership, and without wise leadership terrible things can happen to people who live in these countries. So I hope we will continue to fight for change that will be beneficial to everyone.

Congressman Henry Waxman, thank you very much.